Mastering Sadhana

Mastering Sadhana

On Retreat with Anthony de Mello

CARLOS VALLES, S.J.

AN IMAGE BOOK
Doubleday
New York London Toronto Sydney Auckland

An Image book
Published by Doubleday, a division of Bantam Doubleday Dell Publishing
Group Inc., 666 Fifth Avenue, New York, New York 10103.

Image, Doubleday and the portrayal of a cross
intersecting a circle are trademarks of Doubleday,
a division of Bantam Doubleday Dell Publishing Group, Inc.

Imprimi Potest: A. Sankoorikal, S.J.
Prov. of Gujarat
August 10, 1987

Imprimatur: † C. Gomes, S.J.
Bishop of Ahmedabad
August 12, 1987

ACKNOWLEDGMENTS

The author is grateful for permission to quote from the following:

Simply Sane by Gerald May, © 1976 by Gerald May. Used by permission of Paulist
Press.

Concilium 159 (9/1982).

Freedom from the Known (various pages) by J. Krishnamurti, © 1969 by
Krishnamurti Foundation. Victor Gollancz Ltd., London (1977).

The Wisdom of Insecurity by Alan W. Watts, © 1951, reprinted by permission of
Pantheon Books, a Division of Random House, Inc.

Autobiography by Bertrand Russell, copyright © George Allen & Unwin (Publish-
ers) Ltd., 1967.

Sadhana: A Way to God by Anthony de Mello, S.J., Image Books, Doubleday,
Garden City, N.Y. 1984. Copyright © 1978 by Anthony de Mello.

Library of Congress Cataloging-in-Publication Data

De Mello, Anthony, 1931–
Mastering sadhana.

1. Retreats.   2. Spiritual direction.
I. Vālesa, Father, 1925–   . II. Title.
BX2375.D4 1988   269'.6   88-12743

ISBN 0-385-24581-5

Thinking of you,
Tony,
master and friend

Contents

Contents

To American Readers

In preparing the American edition of this book I am faced with a dilemma. Tony's audiences in India were different from those in America, and consequently the expression of his thought varied also. Should I, then, present to America his thought as he presented it in India, or adapt it to its American version? In India Tony, apart from general workshops or open seminars, worked with small groups for several months together. In America he had much larger audiences and shorter courses. These different settings made for different approaches. When his listeners were few and the courses long, Tony went into details and worked out matters which required time to assimilate as they might be new and unfamiliar to the audience. In a shorter time and with a large audience he could not hope to be able to clarify ideas and clear possible misunderstandings, and so, sensitively, he refrained from touching upon such points.

One such point, and an important one, is the doctrine of the "non-self." Few people in America have heard Tony explain that matter, though that was the center of his latest teaching. To most people it sounds new and strange, and a short exposition could create confusion instead of giving light. A very perceptive American reader who has read this book in typescript (as prepared for the Indian edition) has even suggested the advisability of dropping the whole chapter on "The Self and the Non-Self" from the American edition. When hearing that considered opinion I felt quite ready to suppress the chapter, as I am not attached to what I have written for its own sake. True, the book would then lose its climax, but if by losing it, it gains in clarity and acceptability, I am prepared to let it go. I also feel, however, that dropping this matter altogether would be unfair to Tony, as it evidently meant much to him and gave consistency to his thought and practice. It would also be unfair to American readers who have a right to know Tony's thought in as complete a way as possible. Omission of this point would seriously mutilate Tony's thinking, and, after consideration, I think it better to risk some misunderstanding than to suppress a substantial portion of his teaching.

The chapter, then, stands, as the ideas, the meaning, and the emphasis are Tony's, and so are almost the very words which I took down in detailed notes. It has to be taken in the context I painstakingly elaborate in the whole book, before and after that chapter, to avoid any one-sided interpretation. What would certainly be one-sided, on the other hand, would be to take only the Tony of the large audiences, ignoring the Tony of the small intimate groups. The two aspects of Tony complement and enrich each other, and the specific contribution of this book can be to throw light on the "private" Tony while his books, tapes, and videos focus on the "public" one. If any reader finds any part of this book unhelpful, he or she will do well to ignore it, and give the benefit of the doubt (if any arises) to Tony and, I hope, to me whose only endeavor is to be faithful to Tony's thought.

A similar consideration applies to the words "selfish, greedy, vicious, stupid, innocent, and blameless" which give rise to another difficult chapter. Abstract philosophy was never Tony's strong point, and some of his expressions, if pushed to technical extremes, could cause difficulty. When he stressed a point, he did it so convincingly that an unwary listener might lose sight of the other side of the question, necessary for the proper balance. Tony's dialectics used the "coincidence of opposites" of Nicholas of Cusa, expression which he very often quoted, and to bring it out, he would forcibly present now one extreme, now another (as, in this case, man's freedom and circumstances' conditioning determinism), and leave the listener the task of finding his own balance in the middle. He gave shock treatment to people to shake them out of routine in their thinking as much as in their behavior, but those shock waves must be understood as pedagogical rather than ideological. Readers of this book will, no doubt, exercise the sense we, as listeners, exercised in Lonavla, and place themselves in the right perspective for a balanced view.

I heard Tony say, "Don't give people more than they can take . . . but open a little window that they may think." He did precisely that. Now, it is easy to fix the size of the window in individual counseling or in a small group, difficult in a large group, and impossible in a book that may find its way into anybody's hands. That is why Tony in his books resorted to stories rather than essays, and spoke in parables as Jesus did. I state here in all honesty that I have deliberately left out of this book some things Tony actually said in a small group but, in my judgment, would not have said to a large audience; while, at the same time, I have endeavored to mention all that I felt was truly important in his thought. To draw the line has, at times, not been easy, and I may have erred occasionally on one side or the other. That is the price I have to pay for attempting to describe Tony's teaching systematically, and I am willing to pay the price. Only let not those limiting cases obscure the vision of the whole.

The fact that Tony said things in private which he would not say in public was only practical prudence, and by no means a maneuver to hide doubtful teaching. Tony was a staunch Catholic (in India we say that being a Goan is more, in the scale of orthodoxy, than being a Catholic, and Tony was a Bombay-born Goan!), and his thought was always shaped by his profoundly Christian faith. He dedicated the first of his books to Our Lady, the second to the Church, "Mother and Teacher," and the third to the Jesuit Order, while in its first page he declared himself to be a disciple of Jesus Christ. Precisely because of the great faith he had in his Christian convictions he could go out in sympathy to other doctrines and other experiences and assimilate all that was good and valid in them into his own Catholic practice. He could be openly ecumenical because he was unmistakably Christian.

I am a witness of the special regard and affection Tony had for America and all the people he had come to know and love there, and I want to record it here for the American readers of this book. While I was discussing his plans for 1987 with him, he mentioned that he planned to go twice to the States, once in summer for a number of courses, and once in November, this time only for the very brief but very fruitful ministry of the "Satellite Retreat" where thousands of people heard him live and could ask him questions from all over the United States and Canada. He then added that this would be a very short trip, and that he found that tiring (he disclosed to me that he had to take sleeping pills during his intercontinental plane journeys) and that this particular activity did not bring him much money (which he needed for the building of the new Sadhana Institute); still, he went on, he was undertaking that journey most willingly as a service to his friends in the States "to pay the Americans for all they do for me which is more than I can say." His death in New York links him forever to America in earthly embrace. In that same spirit, and knowing that in doing this I am doing something that would certainly please him, I offer this book to the American readers.

CARLOS G. VALLES, S.J.
St. Xavier's College
Ahmedabad—380 009
India.

Mastering Sadhana

Lonavla

Dear Carlos,

I found your letter to my secretary, and I took it out to answer it myself. I am DELIGHTED that you are coming to Lonavla for the Sadhana renewal in April. I'm planning to work out my latest ideas with the group, and I'm glad you'll be there. From your own Sadhana batch Leela and Joe Puli are coming, and possibly Isabel Alvarez too. You may know some of the others, and in any case you'll all have the common Sadhana background. For the first time you'll have a decent room and a new building thanks to Mario's labours. Come ready for a good time.

Love,

TONY

The letter moved me. I held it in my hand for a time, keeping my eyes on that word "DELIGHTED" in capitals from the recognizable types of his Canon portable electronic typewriter. I was coming to Lonavla for my own needs, and I was made to feel welcome, already before arrival, by a friend who had the gift of making everybody feel that he or she was someone special in his presence. Many men and women across continents will feel that they had a special relationship to Tony, and they are fully right. His ready memory, his warm spontaneity, and, above all, his fundamental capacity to live the present as though nothing else existed or were ever to exist gave to his contact with any person a depth and a glow that lasted long in grateful memory.

Tony and I had met briefly in Vinayalaya and Poona during our studies, and, though the contact was not yet intimate, it was enough to associate in my mind a kind of joyful freshness with the name of Tony de Mello, and to make me react immediately years later when, already a priest and professor in full activity, I happened to read in the Bombay *Jesuit News* that Father Tony de Mello proposed to direct a thirty-day closed Retreat for any Jesuits, young or old, who wished to apply. I wrote on the same day, and he called back long distance from Bombay to Ahmedabad to tell me he was glad I was coming. He had learned from Father Calveras in Spain the original purpose and method of the Spiritual Exercises and was eager, with the zeal and enthusiasm that characterized everything he did, to share with others the joy of his discovery, the proven efficacy of that outstanding means of spiritual renewal.

Already by then he had detractors. I stopped in Bombay for a day on my way to Khandala where the Retreat was to take place, and a senior Jesuit, Rector of one of the houses there, on learning where I was going, had the bad taste to tell me in a rather harsh tone, "Yes, that is all Tony will ever do: talk, talk, talk. Provided he has an audience to listen to him, he is happy; and since he cannot get that here, he has organized that retreat. Imagine! Twenty Jesuits listening to him for a month! Isn't that heaven for him? Go there if you must, but you are wasting your time." I felt sadness and anger at the disgruntled old man who could not stand the initial success of his younger brother. Jealousy runs high among achievers, and Tony was to feel the brunt of it throughout his life. Successes are dearly paid for always.

The Khandala experience had the result of drawing me into the Long-Retreat movement. Tony would get people to invite me to direct Long Retreats for them, and then would get me to accept the invitation. Thus I found myself using the summer (May) and Diwali (October) university holidays to give Long Retreats through the length and breadth of India year after year. That was a most fruitful activity for myself and, I can hope, for others too. Years later, during a concelebrated Eucharist on Tony's birthday at which I was present, he looked at me and said, "One of the things I feel happy about is to have got Carlos involved in the Long-Retreat movement." That involvement brought also, always with Tony, the refreshing experience of the Charismatic movement, which accounted for some of the spiritually happiest years in my life. Eventually the intensity of these two magnificent but, of necessity, transient movements subsided, and I found myself in quest of new directions for my spirit. Tony, always alert and always on the move for new spiritual adventures (he liked to call himself "a rolling stone") had started the Sadhana courses in De Nobili College, Poona. *Sadhana* is a Sanskrit word which can be roughly translated as "spirituality," and which became associated with Tony's work and person. When an impatient inquirer asked a friend of mine, "Tell me once and for all what is this Sadhana!" my friend answered, "Sadhana is Tony, and Tony is Sadhana."

At about that time my Provincial (none other than Father Joe Aizpun, who was later to join Tony in the staff of the

Sadhana Institute in Lonavla and become its religious Superior) told me, "You know that Tony is running now these
Sadhana courses in Poona. You are very much in contact
with young Jesuits, and I am interested in their getting
proper inspiration and guidance. You could help in that
task, and, to equip you better for it, I have thought of sending you for the Sadhana course. I have spoken to Tony
about it, and he has told me he will make room for you in
any course you care to attend. Now, you have a choice.
They have at present the 'mini-Sadhana,' which is just one
month, and the 'maxi-Sadhana,' which takes nine full
months. I know that you are busy with your teaching in the
university, and so I leave the choice to you, even the choice
to go or not to go at all. But I'll be happy if you go at least
for the short one." Joe and I had been friends since Spain,
and so I took the liberty to answer him with a Gospel quotation: "Joe, we have been so many years together, and you
don't know me yet? You know well that for me there are no
'minis.' I never do things by halves. Either I do the whole
thing, or I leave it altogether. No mini-Sadhanas for me. Put
my name down for the 'maxi,' this very year." I took a
sabbatical from my university teaching and went to Poona
full of eagerness.

Tony sensed my eagerness and set about calming it down
from the beginning. In the first meeting with the group he
announced that the sessions would begin at ten—"Well,
let's say 'tennish' to keep it informal"—there was not to be
a fixed agenda, and we would proceed as we felt our way
along. I remonstrated with all the weight that being the
seniormost in the group gave me: "Tony, I value my time,
I've made a big sacrifice coming here, and I want to know
what I am going to do these nine months. I need a clear
syllabus and a fixed timetable so that I can work with full
earnestness from the beginning." Tony listened to me indul-
gently and dismissed my query with a purposely patronizing

gesture: "O Carlos, don't worry; you'll change." The group laughed, and I was left fuming. Therapy had begun. I did change, and I came to regard that year, as I have heard most people who have passed through it declare, as the most important of my life.

One year, however intense, is not enough, and soon Tony organized the Renewals. Fifteen days in October or April when anybody who had gone through any Sadhana course could relive the atmosphere that had fostered his first change, and charter new advances. By then the Institute had moved to Lonavla amid the dilapidated austerity of a summer villa and the dreadful bites of the outsize mosquitoes that infest the countryside. It is no small compliment to Tony and his staff that they endured year after year the permanent hardship of temporary housing; and in fact that circumstance was mentioned, to their credit, in the official report ordered by the authorities. I attended two such Renewals in Lonavla, and, when taking leave of Tony after the second, I told him half in jest that I would come again only when the new building was ready.

That was in 1987. The Renewal was announced to take place from March 30 to April 14. The staff quarters, guest rooms, kitchen, dining room, and main halls were already up and ready for use. The truth is that I had decided to go in any case, as I had passed through troubled times and felt the need of regaining the peace and balance which experience had led me to associate with Sadhana. I applied at once, and the answer was the letter I have printed here. On March 30 the Sadhana van, another welcome addition to the complex, picked me up from the Lonavla railway station and took me to the new premises. Twenty-five men and women were ready for the course.

Then a strange thing happened. So strange and so much out of character with me that I have hesitated long before writing it here. Some readers, I fear, will be negatively af-

fected by it, and in any case it will easily look like manufac-
tured hindsight or comfortable prophecy after the events.
Still, the feeling was absolutely strong and clear within me,
it lasted through all those days and it has a direct bearing on
this book, so that I feel I owe it to myself and to my readers
to set it down here. The fact is that soon after my arrival
there (I cannot pinpoint the exact moment or occasion, but
it was very early in the course) I got an uncanny feeling, a
definite premonition or foreboding that Tony was going to
die after the Renewal and that this last course was going to
be his spiritual testament to us. It sounded ridiculous and I
never mentioned it to anyone, but the feeling never left me
and led me to a very concrete action, without which this
book would not have been possible. I had not planned to
take any notes during the course, as I knew Tony well
enough by then, and I thought that the direct listening to
him, drinking in his ideas, and imbibing the whole atmosphere created by his talks was all that I needed to quiet and
strengthen my soul. But when this strange conviction that
this was going to be Tony's testament took hold of me, I
borrowed paper (strangely I, who never go anywhere without paper, had brought none with me this time as I did not
mean to use any) and started taking detailed notes at every
session. Those notes will form the basis of this book.

These notes are of course my notes, filtered through my
own brain and conditioned by my own understanding of
Tony. Tony used to say that when he gave a talk to a hundred persons he gave a hundred different talks, as each one
understood his words according to his or her own precon-
ceived ways of thinking. Water takes the shape of the vessel
it fills. I am well aware of that, and one day in Lonavla I
made a little experiment. Tony had been dialoging with us
for about an hour and a half, and then called for a recess. By
my side sat a Sister who had been taking notes as devotedly
as myself. I asked her, with the easy confidence that Sadhana

generates in all its participants, "Sister, shall we exchange notes? I'm curious to see what you have written about Tony's talk, as also to know what you think about what *I* have written." She smiled and handed me her notebook. Fortunately hers was a woman's clear and beautiful handwriting, and I went fast through her pages. She had more trouble with mine, as I had sacrificed legibility to speed (in that I follow Beethoven's dictum that "life is too short to spend it in leisurely handwriting"). I watched her with an expectant smile till she finished. Then she looked up at me, and we both burst simultaneously into laughter. We knew why we were laughing. Our notes were so different that if a third person had read them, not knowing that they proceeded from the same talk, he would have thought the notes belonged to two entirely different talks. She had taken down in her own way what had struck her, and I had taken down in my own way what had struck me; and since we were quite different persons, our notes were also quite different.

I am the first to recognize this limitation, and I clearly set it down here at the outset. But then, with the same sincerity, I want to state my claim to a fair approximation to Tony's thought. I do so by quoting his words to me on an occasion too important to me ever to fade from my memory. In one of my Renewals with him, after a long personal talk between both of us alone in which I reviewed for his comments all my spiritual trajectory since my first Sadhana, he told me these exact words: "Many people have passed through my hands, Carlos, but you are the only person who has fully understood me and my principles to their ultimate consequences." I knew what he meant, and treasured the compliment. This by no means makes me a perfect "Sadhanite" or gives me preference in any way above anybody else. It would be foolish of me even to think that. I have also heard Tony single out by name some men and women as having profited specially by Sadhana while he left out my name. Let all be clearly said. The outcome to me is that without rankings or preferences, and within the essential limitations inherent in the task of a man reproducing another man's thought, I may be allowed to trust that my attempt to interpret Tony will not be unworthy of him.

He himself told me in Lonavla while I was encouraging him to set down systematically in a formal book all his thought and experience, "I am not a writer. I am a storyteller, and that is the way they introduce me in America: Father Anthony de Mello the storyteller. I write stories and meditations, but not essays or treatises. My writing is open-ended . . . and let the reader draw his own conclusions." He even joked with me then in Spanish, which he knew perfectly well, and in which he also knew that the word "storyteller" is translated by *cuentista,* which also means "bluffer." He was ready to apply both meanings to himself. This, of course, piles up one more difficulty before my undertaking. I am getting down to describing rather systematically the thought of a man who refused to do that himself. Those who knew him will be able to translate back in their minds from statement to story and draw their own conclusions as Tony would have liked them to do.

Tony said openly that each one of his courses, workshops, conferences, was as much for himself as for the participants. He grew through them, clarified his thoughts, sharpened his feelings, tempered his mind . . . and, of course, enjoyed himself immensely. He put himself heart and soul into every exchange, and developed his gifts by using them. He used to say that if others had done Sadhana for one month, six months, nine months, he was doing it for a lifetime. He learned by doing. And it is in this same spirit that I have undertaken to write this book. By writing about Tony's teachings I want to assimilate them deeper myself. When I took leave of him in April he told me, "Do come again next year for the Renewal. We must make it a point to meet every year, Carlos." I assured him I had every intention to come again, and he knew I meant it.

Now there will be no more Renewals with Tony. All I am left with (apart, of course, from what has already gone happily into my system) are my memories and my notes. I want to make the best of them, and so I have set myself the task of reading them again and again, loving them, assimilating them, putting some order into them, and setting them out finally in this book. Thus the book is meant for me as much as for anybody else. This exercise is healing and guidance of the first kind for me in my own persisting needs. Whatever these pages do for others, they will renew in me the fruit which I went to seek in Lonavla, and which I summed up in this way to Tony on the last day of the Renewal: "I have found this time in Sadhana joyful reassurance in my way of life; greater clarity to see, and strength to live, in a measure far beyond my expectations." If writing is therapy, this book is my Sadhana.

Bombshells

He didn't give us a chance. I had expected, and others with
me, that Tony would start the proceedings with the usual
question: "What do you propose we do in these fifteen
days?" The men and women of the group were all well
versed in the Sadhana ways, and could be relied upon to
respond at once with concrete suggestions and personal
needs, most of them thought up in advance, out of which
Tony would pick up converging lines and plan the sessions.
But this time he did nothing of the kind. Or rather, yes, he
asked the question, but only in an academic way, through a
mere "exercise" without follow-up. He ordered us, "Each
one of you find a congenial partner; team up with him or
her, and tell each other what you expect from these days."
We did as commanded, but then he did not ask us to bring
out our requests before the group or before him in any way.
He just ignored the exercise and went on to give us another
one . . . not without a touch of humor.

The order came: "Divide yourselves into groups of five, in such a way that the five of you in each group like each other and get on well together. Quick!" There was the regular scramble that followed such orders, of which we all had already good experience. The anxiety not to be left alone, the instant search, the risk to approach someone who may in perfect freedom say no, the fun to be pulled by two people in two directions, the final adjustments when a group finds itself with six members and another with four, and the end result of the groups standing separately, five groups of five to account exactly for the twenty-five of us. There was expectation in the air to see what kind of game we would now be asked to play and where it would lead us by way of beginning the first lesson. "Now each group give itself a name to be called by." My group did me the honor of calling itself by my name: Carlos. The honor, however, did not last long. Tony announced with mock solemnity, "These groups will take care, by turn, of the washing up after meals and the peeling of potatoes and onions in the kitchen every morning." The game was over. We all laughed happily and sat down again. Then Tony began.

"I know what I want to do this time with you. I have reached an important moment in my life when many of my ideas have changed and I feel the need to clarify them to myself, test them and express them. For that I need the group. I will bring up a point each morning, then you react, ask any questions you want, connected or not connected with it, and we'll see where we go from there. You may expect some bombshells. I have a few ready for you."

I was thrilled to hear him speak that way. That Tony changed his ideas was no secret to those who knew him. He had begun by telling us, years before, "If you follow what I say, you do it at your own risk, because I can change my views without notice." Some people held that against him, and he himself quoted such cases. In previous years, while directing thirty-day Retreats, he had emphasized total poverty, not only in inner detachment but in actual practice. Some people, inspired by his teaching, had given up all comforts and embraced a truly austere life; and when Tony later changed gears ("I realized that my 'poverty' had become my 'riches,' that is, that I was attached to my image as a poor man and full of pride for it, so that poverty had defeated its purpose"), those people felt let down and some resented him. He was not affected by such criticism. He always advocated a simple life and inner detachment, and if anybody, under his previous influence, had gone to extremes, that was his concern.

He knew his own powers of persuasion and warned us against them. "Don't let yourselves be hypnotized by me," he would say at times. He reminded me of those scholastic dialecticians in the Middle Ages who, for lack of a better entertainment, would set up a pulpit in a public square, defend for a length of time any proposition against all objectors, and then change and defend the opposite view with the same success. Tony would perform a similar feat in "role-playing," where, acting as counselee he made his problem appear absolutely insoluble, and then shifting places and acting as counselor he showed a reasonable and perfectly simple way out of the difficulty. In any case he had a truly open mind and a great inner freedom which permitted him to accept a new view when he was convinced of its legitimacy.

He had begun to use the terminology "Sadhana I" for his views of ten or twelve years ago, and "Sadhana II" for his present views. He had been changing all along, but now he saw a clear divide, and the very contrast was helping his thinking. And the promise he now held out to us was nothing less than the adventure of going into Sadhana II from the basis of Sadhana I, which we all knew well. In other words, to follow Tony in his own voyage of discovery through moods and insights. There was no question of knowing "the latest Tony" out of mere curiosity, or even derisive irony—as some people who appreciated him less would say, "Come, let's hear what Tony's latest craze is." For us in that opening day of the Lonavla experience, certainly for me, who had followed Tony's turns of mind with friendly respect and personal profit, that was a precious opportunity to learn at the source new points of view and recent experiences which were sure to be serious and practical, and probably far-reaching in their consequences. My personal feeling at that moment was one of gentle elation and expectation after that promising opening. I knew that when Tony had taken such a clear initiative, he would live up to it. I told myself, "I'm lucky to be here."

That Tony needed the group to clarify his own ideas was also known to us all. He needed the sounding board, the reactions, the instant feedback. He was at his best when he listened intently to a query, looked away for an instant in obvious concentration, then faced the person (sometimes bodily, getting up from his place, dragging his own chair, and sitting directly in front of the victim, to everybody's amusement and his or her apprehensive embarrassment) and started a sharp dialogue which was sure to pinpoint and clarify the issue for everyone, including himself. He knew he functioned best in the group, and, while he was ready to counsel anybody in private and was overwhelmingly generous with his time for anybody who needed it, he clearly had told us from the beginning that he preferred us to bring even our personal problems to him in the presence of the group, as he could deal better with them there. He referred to that situation as "the football-match effect." A player in a friendly match without spectators is not likely to give of his best, but in a keen competition in a large stadium full of cheering fans, he is sure to strain every nerve and employ every resource beyond even his ordinary capacity. That happened definitely to him, and now that there was a question of revising his own mental setup he wanted to do it in and with the group, and in fact had been waiting for this opportunity to do it. At the end of the experience he said publicly that he had liked the group and found it very helpful.

There was another circumstance that was going to make this meeting special. The teaching staff of Sadhana was made up of Tony de Mello, Joe Aizpun, and Dick McHugh (together with the gifted and efficient Mario Correa to look after everything else). However, on this occasion Dick was still recovering from a stubborn disease, and Joe was visiting Jesus-and-Mary convents throughout India in a spiritual-renewal tour. That had left us with Tony alone for the fifteen days. We felt the loss, since Joe and Dick, with their very different and complementary approaches, always contributed greatly to the richness of the Sadhana experience. But there was also a positive consideration to offset the loss: By having Tony alone for that length of time and at that important moment, we would concentrate intensely and exclusively on all that he wanted to communicate to us, and this very concentration was likely to create a single-mindedness and purposefulness in all of us to help faster understanding and assimilation. This was what happened in fact. The unalloyed exposure to Tony twenty-four hours a day for fifteen days created an atmosphere where every moment echoed the same tune and every incident pointed to the same aim, and even an informal conversation reflected the proceedings of the last session. I told Tony at the end, "I have profited more by these fifteen days than by the nine months before." An exaggeration, of course, but also a genuine expression of my mood at the time. Everything had contributed to make it a memorable occasion.

The timetable was easy to fix. In the morning, sessions with intervals from nine to twelve-thirty; in the afternoon, after rest, he would have private interviews or walks with individual persons; and in the evening, the concelebrated

Eucharist at which he himself took daily the place of the main concelebrant. For good measure, at night after supper we watched several days the videos of his American talks, particularly the one of his "satellite Retreat," which was repeated by popular request. He himself watched them sometimes with us, and enlivened the show with his commentaries. "See how I look like an idiot, just to feign innocent ignorance before that question which is a risky one." "But what the hell am I doing there with that glass of water in my hand, neither drinking it nor putting it down? I must remember not to do that again." "And that word now, well, it escaped me. It is one of the words banned from official television. The technicians looked at each other in horror when I said it, but anyway the show was live and there was nothing they could do. They told me later that they had not thought it necessary to inform me about the forbidden words. If they only knew the language I use! After that I was more careful." And so the whole day. Even at meals we had his witty, teasing, boisterous presence which made it impossible for anybody to forget for a moment that he was around. We truly had him in full measure to ourselves, and I want to record here the unstinting generosity with which he gave himself to us in those exceptional days.

At the daily Eucharist he was the only one to speak, and when, after some days, he asked us whether we wanted a change, we unanimously asked him to continue that way. That was no laziness on our part, or refusal to share in the work, but a clear expression of the satisfaction we all experienced when we saw him winding up in prayer and Eucharist the themes he had dealt with during the day. The rubric was simple and touching. He read out slowly two meditations from a book he was preparing, each followed by a long silence under the melodies of the Pan flute which he loved and selected carefully for his tape recorder. I noticed an industrious Sister who kept taking notes on the sly while

Tony talked during the Mass, eager not to miss a single word for her own record. I approached her after the last blessing when she was still with her notebook on her lap and the pen in her hand, and asked her with awe, "Do you take down all that Tony says at Mass?" She answered demurely, "Yes; it helps me." I urged, "Even when he says, 'Blessed are you, Lord, God of all creation . . .', do you take that down too?" She smiled her embarrassment but went on writing. Each one was trying to profit the most in his or her own way. I did not take down those meditations, and so I shall not include them here.

In his introduction that first morning Tony repeated the word "bombshells," raising his voice and shaking his head for greater effect. "Yes, yes . . . bombshells . . . they're surely coming. Get ready!" It was clear that whatever Tony intended to say those days, it was important to him.

To Change or Not to Change

"I used to tell you before: Change! Change for the sake of changing. So long as you don't have a strong reason not to change, change! Change is growth and change is life; so if you want to keep alive, keep on changing. Well, now I tell you: Don't change. Change is impossible, and even if it were possible, it is undesirable. Stay as you are. Love yourselves as you are. And change, if it is at all possible, will take place by itself when and if it wants. Leave yourselves alone."

That was quite a change in Tony, good itself for a paradox! All his life he had been a most ardent apostle of change, placing it at the root af all advance and all progress in personal growth and in spiritual life. And now suddenly he changed gears and stopped all change. Roundabout turn. He had changed to tell us we shouldn't change. Adding, to make it clear, that change would then come by itself, which is the only true change. A bit of a confusion. And Tony

enjoyed creating confusion, out of which light eventually
was bound to come. The idea is in fact simpler than it seems,
though it is definitely important.

Tony's main objection to change was now that when we
set ourselves to change ourselves or others, we do so out of
intolerance (and that, of course, cannot be tolerated!). We
cannot bear with a shortcoming, a defect, a moral or psychological weakness in ourselves, and we set about correcting it
with hidden spite and ill-concealed violence. We seek to
change in order to be accepted, to conform to expectations,
to live up to the ideal image we have made up for ourselves.
We are impatient with ourselves, and so we want to force
ourselves to change. That, of course, will never do. No
growth ever results from violence.

The only growth-promoting change is that which comes
from self-acceptance. Change can never be forced; it occurs.
The paradox of change is that it is only by forgetting it that
it can ever take place, if it does at all. Resistance to ourselves, to anything in ourselves, only serves to strengthen
that which we are resisting, and thus makes change impossible.

I illustrate the principle with my own case. I had come to
Lonavla because I was too tense and wanted to unwind.
Several factors in my recent past had contributed to over-
load my already taut nerves, and I found myself irritable,
jumpy, uneasy, resenting people, and losing my sleep. I had
planned to tell Tony this in the presence of the group and
let him work on me with therapy, counseling, exercises, or
any of the untold resources he had at his disposal to set me
on the healing way. I was tense, and was relying on Tony to
help me stop being tense. Instead of that he told me coolly
when I brought up my problem in the group, "So you are
tense, Carlos. That's fine. Accept the fact that you are tense.
Your tension may or may not go during these days. If it
goes, it's fine, and if it remains, it's fine. Happiness is some-

thing more than feeling no tension, as life is something more than health. You may be happy while you are tense, and perfectly relaxed but unhappy. You don't even know whether it is good for you to be tense or not to be tense. So leave it alone. Just get into life, into the sessions, into whatever you do here, and let your nerves go their way. Nature is wise and can take care of itself if only you allow it. The less you interfere, the better."

I saw the wisdom in the advice. I was tense and wanted to force myself to relax. That, of course, increased the tension. How shall I relax? How long will it take me? What will happen to me if I don't succeed in relaxing? Madness upon madness. Paradoxically the only way for me to relax was to allow myself to be tense. Yes, I'm tense, and it's fine with me. I've given myself permission to be tense. Now what? Who is there to complain? What is wrong with being tense? I've been tense all my life and it hasn't been a bad life in any case. I can go on in the same way for as long as I live. Tense people of the world, unite! Let us fight for our rights and defend our way of life! There is a place for us in this world, and we want to occupy it with dignity. Long live our nerves!

Tony even said about himself with characteristic humility (which in him was matter-of-fact realism), "Formerly as therapist I communicated intolerance and led the person to reject himself." The urge to change, to do better, to imitate those in the group who "made the grade" and were secretly held up as models to all the others, the need to be able to say "I have changed" and make the group recognize it . . . all that could weigh heavily on the mind and do more harm than good. Toward the end of the nine-month Sadhana we all wrote evaluations of one another and shared them together. The greatest praise one could hope for in those evaluations was to be told, "You have changed a lot." That pressure to change, while no change was forthcoming, did create problems and may have led at times to frustration and self-rejection.

One thing I already did notice in the first Sadhana, and I commented it in the group toward the end of the course. When we began the nine months, each one of us was bringing up his or her personal problems for solution. To take a very innocent example, a man would say that he blushed when he was introduced to another person, and wanted to get rid of his blushing. Tony would set to work with him in full earnest. Counseling, therapy, exercises, role-playing. Time passed and the blushing remained. (I cannot think of a single "problem" that was "solved" that year.) When the nine months were coming to an end, our man would bring up his case again and make a last attempt to stop blushing. Then Tony's approach changed radically. He would face him and tell him squarely, "Are you ready to live with your problem?" If you cannot change it, accept it. Then the very acceptance will pave the way for the change, if it is to come at all. The difference in Tony's approach was that now he began where he formerly ended. Accept the facts, reconcile yourself to the situation, be at peace with yourself . . . and change will take care of itself.

The following story does not come from Tony, but I read it during those days at Lonavla and it throws light on the psychological truth that by resisting an unwelcome trait in our character we rather aggravate it. A psychiatrist reports the case of a man who came to him with a stammering problem. He could not open his mouth without stammering badly, and that was the way it had been with him all his life. The psychiatrist asked him, "Can you remember at least an occasion in your life when you spoke without stammering?" Yes, there was one. The stammerer told the story that once as a young man he had boarded a bus in a hurry without a ticket, and was worried thinking what would happen when the conductor came along to check his ticket. Then he thought, "When he comes, I'll start to explain my situation, and since I stammer so badly he'll have pity on me and will let me off." In fact he was planning to exaggerate his stammer so as to make his appeal for mercy more effective. The conductor approached, the stammerer rehearsed his act, opened his mouth . . . and speech came out without a flaw in rapid, neat pronunciation. The conductor smiled knowingly at the "fake" stammerer and imposed his fine. Our man's discomfiture was complete. For once his stammering could have been of use to him, and it had let him down!

That was precisely the point. So long as the man resisted his stammer, the stammer persisted. Why should this happen to me? How can I live with this? How can I meet people? How can I get a job if I speak in this way? How long will it last? Everything in him protested against the unfair and painful situation. And that only increased the evil. He stammered all the more . . . and he resented it all the more. A vicious circle difficult to break. But for once he found himself feeling happy that he was a stammerer, he rejoiced that his stammer was going to get him out of his difficulty as a ticketless traveler, he even tried to increase his stammer and make it more evident. And the stammer vanished. For the single occasion in his life when he accepted his stammer, the stammer disappeared. That is a striking illustration of the way human nature works. It will resist with all its might any direct attempt to change it, while it will change by itself when left alone or even prodded in the other direction. Donkeys do exactly the same.

When the urge to change is applied not to change oneself but to change others, it becomes even more deadly, and Tony warned us heavily against it. We want the other man to change, for his own good, of course! He would be so much happier if he did. Now he makes a nuisance of himself to everybody, he impairs his own work, he does not allow his own good qualities to appear because of those silly defects which everybody knows in him and which he alone seems not to notice. I must tell him, I must urge him, I must face him with the facts to make him correct himself; or, if I cannot do that, I must at least pray to God that he may change him for the good of all.

Please, don't say that prayer. Such a prayer is only your camouflaged rejection of your brother. Do pray for him, and thank the Lord for him, but don't ask him to change him in the way you had planned for him. It is not for you to judge, to condemn, and to prescribe change. Leave your brother alone, even in your thoughts of him, and accept him and love him as he is. The desire to change others, as the desire to change oneself, comes basically from intolerance, and that is why it is vitiated at the source. Change, if it does not come out of intolerance, is welcome; but, as often as not, there is an element of intolerance in it, and this is what we have to be warned against.

Tony said, "Do you imagine how happy our groups, our families, our communities would be if everybody in them would stop trying to change everybody else, would stop even wishing them to change? They would become heaven in one day. But we are always complaining within us, and often to others, about the behaviour of the rest of us, and that intolerance destroys the harmony of our group life." In our Lonavla batch there was a Jesuit Provincial who told me, "When my subjects come to talk to me they spend most of their time telling me what I must do about other subjects, how I must correct them, check them, forbid them to do this or command them to do that. Everybody seems to know perfectly well what everybody else has to do; and everybody wants to see the law enforced . . . but on the others; not precisely on himself." Our very desire for self-improvement has sharpened severely our sense of criticism, and it now stands in the way of the very improvement we want for ourselves and for others. It is time we broaden our outlook and make acceptance, instead of criticism, the basis of our behavior with others . . . and with ourselves.

Behind this practical attitude there is a deep religious truth. It is God who has made me, made others, and made the world, and therefore acceptance of the reality that is in me and around me is acceptance of God's will and worship of his Divine Majesty. Through all the pain and suffering of mankind, through all the sin of man and the calamities of nature, the fact of faith is that this universe, with me in it, is the work of God; and therefore the best and only way for me to enter into it and work out my salvation through it is to accept it as God's gift to me, see him in all things and all men, and let him work though me with his power and his grace under my gratitude and cooperation. God's own opinion of the world he created is that it was "very good indeed," and the presence in it later of his People, his Son and his Church, made it an even more lovable place. *"Mirabiliter creasti et mirabilius reformasti"* ("a wonderful creation, and an even more wonderful redemption"). We seem to have forgotten the wonder and be left only with the misery. Let us recover the full-faith vision of the world, which includes the Cross and also the Resurrection. We are the members of the risen Christ, and we have to learn to rejoice together with our head. To look at life with the eyes of God is to accept it, and that is the first step in sanity and in grace. We are on solid ground.

Acceptance of reality does not in any way mean conformism, passivity, apathy. For anybody who knew Tony it will be just impossible to associate any of those words with him. We accept reality as the bird accepts its wings: to fly. The point is not to start complaining about the type of wings and comparing them with those of other birds, only to remain ultimately on the ground. Acceptance is not inertia, it is joyful recognition of all that is, in order to make the best of things as they are and of life as it is. This may imply initia-

tive and action to influence decisions and change circumstances. If I recognize a seed as a seed, I am getting ready to
water it; if I recognize a sickness as a sickness, I at once go
to the doctor and get my medicine; if I recognize injustice as
injustice, I bestir myself to fight oppression and establish
justice. Recognition of reality, acceptance, and awareness
are no invitation to complacency, but the best invitation to
personal growth and social change. Psychology does not oppose but reinforces sociology.

The book *I'm O.K., You're O.K.* by Thomas Harris had a
good deal of influence on the early stages of Sadhana, and
its terminology passed into Sadhana language. The ultimate
aim among us was "to be O.K.," and the final disgrace "not
to be O.K.". We strove manfully for "O.K.-ness", and we
felt miserable when in spite of all our efforts we failed to
achieve the lofty state. The confession "I'm not O.K." was
like the contrite expression of a public sinner before the
assembly of the just. It called for compassion and penance.
The tyranny of the "O.K." was, in hindsight, one of the
unhappy burdens of the first Sadhana. That is why it was so
refreshing to hear now Tony say, "The theory of *I'm O.K.
You're O.K.* is deadly teaching. It imposes on you the obligation to feel O.K., and unless you feel O.K. there is something wrong with you. That is simply intolerable. I am whatever I am, and I feel whatever I feel, and it's fine. I need not
be O.K. in order to be O.K. if you follow me; I may not be
O.K., and that is perfectly O.K. with me. You must break
free from the O.K. trap. In fact I plan to write someday a
book with the title, *I'm an Ass, You're an Ass* which will be
the antidote to the O.K. doctrine. Someone has already suggested to me a subtitle for the book: *A book you'll get a kick
out of!* Just wait for it."

There is wisdom in the humor. Once I cheerfully accept
that I am an ass, I am not surprised or pained at the silly
things I keep doing in spite of long training and painstaking

efforts. After all, I'm an ass, and if I do stupid things, that was only to be expected of me. In the same way everybody around me is an ass, and so naturally they all behave like the asses they are and will always be, and they have full right to do so. This is the perfect attitude for peace of soul with oneself and with others. Full acceptance of myself as I am and of all others as they are removes tensions and sows happiness. It's a pity Tony will never write that book.

To Love or Not to Love

Another essential axis of Sadhana was relationships. Our affective side had not been much developed in our early religious training, and to make us come alive Tony encouraged us to allow ourselves to feel affection, to express feelings, to form relationships, which, through shyness, doubts, jealousy, and care, would shape us into more complete human beings. For that reason he admitted both men and women to his courses. We had given almost exclusive importance to the intellect, and it was time to bring feelings into the picture to make it more colorful. "I think" became a bad word around there, while "I feel" was the accepted way to begin any statement . . . though sometimes this was only a verbal substitution, and the thinking activity continued unimpaired under the cover of feelings.

Tony's argument ran along these lines: What we ultimately desire is freedom in our behavior and in our hearts; we cannot launch into freedom unless we have a large degree of security in our lives; in order to feel secure we have to feel O.K. (this was Sadhana I); and the only way really to feel O.K. is to feel accepted and loved as persons. Thus the whole emphasis was on receiving love. "Take it in" was the password. The essence of Christianity, Tony went on, is to be able to say from the heart, "God loves me." Paul declared, "He loved me"; and John defined himself as "the disciple whom Jesus loved." A Christian is a person who can truly say, "Jesus loves me." And now, twisting gently and not unworthily John's words, "If I don't experience the love of my brother whom I see, how can I experience the love of God whom I don't see?"

Achievement and success in life do not give security; on the contrary, they undermine it and generate anxiety. The more I succeed, the more I feel the need to keep on succeeding to come up to the expectations I have generated; and so anxiety sets in, increases, and becomes unbearable. Success in work without an affective balance that may offset its bias is the dangerous way to a breakdown for the compulsive worker. Beethoven suffered because people appreciated his music but not his person. Success tells me that my work is fine, while love tells me that *I* am fine, and this is the ultimate satisfaction of the person. I want to be loved for my own sake, not for my music or my books or my works or my organizations. I want to feel affection, to know tenderness, to deserve love. It is this experience of love that gives me a sense of worth, a motive to live and a reason to stand with confidence as a human person in the midst of society.

The depth of true love is that it is unconditional, and is in no way affected by my successes or failures in my work or in my endeavors. When I see myself loved in that way by a friend, I experience the security, the safety, the satisfaction of being loved for my own sake, and therefore not depending on my achievements for my well-being, which is an immense relief. Hence the advice: Love others, experience their love in return, and . . . "take it in!" That will give you joy, balance, and peace.

That was beautiful teaching, to be sure. Still, even there Tony now introduced important modifications. First he toned down the importance of being loved and shifted it to actively loving others. What is important is not that I am loved and accepted, but that I accept and love others. Waiting for others to love me makes me dependent on them, and so jeopardizes my security, whereas loving them on my own is always in my hand and makes me independent and free. A member of the Lonavla group, much respected by all, brought up his problem: "I am not accepted by my community." Tony answered curtly, "Why do you need to be accepted by them? If they accept you, it's fine; and if they don't, it's fine too. Do appreciate their acceptance if they give it to you, but don't beg for it if they don't. Acceptance or no acceptance, you are fine. Paradoxically again this is the best way eventually to obtain their acceptance if it is to come at all."

Then came a deeper reflection: We never really love a person, but the image of the person we have created in our own minds. That was disturbingly true. I feel a great affection for a friend, so much so that I ask myself with genuine surprise, How is it that other people don't love this man as I do, being such a wonderful person as he is? The answer is that he is a wonderful person, no doubt, but it does not appear so to others, while it appears so powerfully and overwhelmingly to me. I have idealized him in my mind and I love and worship that extraordinary image . . . which to others does not look so extraordinary after all. If I loved the man as he is in reality and as he is seen by everybody, then everybody would love him equally, which is not the case. So it is the image, not the person, that I really love.

Then comes the crisis. When that person, whom I had idealized in my mind, loses, through age or routine or just closer contact, the qualities that had attracted me to him, I feel shaken and confused. Do I love him still? Do I not? Of course, I feel it my duty to keep loving him, as a friend has to be loyal, and love eternal, and so I conjure up the old treasured image in my mind while forcibly closing my eyes to the present inferior reality and keep telling myself and him in futile exercise that of course I love him and will always love him forever. Tony mused, with a dry irony which, for once, almost bordered on cynicism, though tempered by his unfailing sense of humor, "You see, married people find this out much faster than we religious do. A man and a woman fall in love (with their respective images, of course), marry, and since they now live together all the time, they soon discover the reality behind the glamour and wonder what they have done. They are now united by the bond, and family and society help them to stay together (at least in some cultures), but they know very well that their mutual love is not anymore what it had appeared in the beginning and promised to be forever. We religious particularly in a man-woman friendship, meet, of necessity, much less, and so the illusion lasts longer. But eventually we too find out, and what had been a thrill becomes a burden. The universal folklore about love, fidelity, and romance, which we too have imbibed, prevents us from seeing this and admitting it to ourselves, but that is the case. This does not mean that friendship is not possible, but that it has to be radically purified."

He quoted cases. As a young man he had been very strongly attracted to a person. They met again only many years later, and Tony exclaimed to himself, "How can I have ever felt anything for a person so odd and unattractive and grumpy?" The contrast between the ideal image he had formed and preserved in his mind and the faded reality he met today made him reflect, as he always did after every experience, on the true nature of human love. On another occasion he was initiating a relationship with a fellow Jesuit, when he came to know that he was not a priest but a lay brother (who is a full-fledged member of the order with the same rights and respect as any other, but without priestly studies or ordination). Immediately he sensed his interest for him diminish, and was almost angry with himself for that. Tony appreciated lay brothers immensely, and some of them were his personal friends; why then should the difference in status affect an incipient relationship? That reminded me of another Jesuit who told me he had been specially friendly with a Jesuit companion, till the day he came to know accidentally that he belonged to a lower caste. Whom do we love, the person or the image?

Another important consideration: None of our loves in this life is purely altruistic; there is always some element of self-regard, of self-gratification, in them. The purest love down here on earth brings benefits of companionship, warmth, pleasure, help, and support which, while perfectly legitimate and valid, are also affected by a touch of self-interest. Tony's conclusion, however, was not to deride friendship and stop love, but to clarify issues and to call things by their names. "You can do whatever you want provided you know what you are doing and call it by its name." Which again does not mean we have to go around telling people "I love the image I have of you" or "in loving you I am also to some extent loving myself"; we can continue to use normal language in the normal way; the only requirement is that in our own minds we must be fully clear about our motives and our intentions. "I know that in loving you I am loving the image I have myself formed about you"; "I realize that my love for you, though fundamentally selfless and pure, includes also a certain amount of gratification of the self-centered attraction I feel for you." This will temper emotions, but will in the long run make for healthier and more lasting relationships. Inner transparency is essential for any deep human contact.

Tony had some very close friendships with a few men and women, and very warm relationships with many more. Still his personal affective life remained veiled by his own restraint and, maybe, his own paradoxical shyness. For all his open laughter and his noisy banter, there was always a deep layer of untouched privacy within him which was never laid bare, and which zealously kept forever the secret of his intimate affective life. The following testimony throws beautiful light on Tony's personality in this most delicate aspect of his relationships.

Tony's colleague, Joe Aizpun, wrote in a sensitive obituary note:

I shall remember Tony first and foremost as a friend. I have not known many people who delighted so much in friendship. He was touchingly proud of his friends, at times delightfully boastful of them. He shared intensely the joys of friends, and when we came to him in moments of difficulty he offered us a warm understanding, wisdom and support which were distinctly and uniquely Tony's. And yet, to many of us, his friends, Tony remained something of a mystery. Was he, deep down, rather a shy person? Did we, his friends, thrust on him so much the role of helper and guide that he found it difficult to be freely his own vulnerable self? He could confess to his vulnerability, talk about it, but rarely did he show it. And so in some ways he was remote. He could be gregarious, he was always the life of a party, he was outrageously humorous, he was incredibly, almost inhumanly available to those who needed him. But for all that, one sensed that he often retired to some private depth into which few, if any, ever entered. Was that because he was so relentlessly true to his own vision? Was it because his life was so much the inner search which, in the end, one can only undertake alone? To many of us Tony was also a wisdom figure. He felt intensely the need to share, to communicate his vision. Many caught

glimpses of it and experienced healing, a new meaning, a new hope.
But I suspect that few really saw what Tony saw, and deep down
Tony knew it. Yet he was never bitter or frustrated, nor was he
condescending in a kind of wiser-than-thou attitude. But I think
that he often felt alone in his search. He went on because he was
possessed by an awesome need to know and to experience for himself.
And he was rewarded with a unique sense of the ecstasy of life, and,
even before he died, of the ecstasy of death too.

Speaking of relationships, and to illustrate the principle
that we always treat others the way we treat ourselves, Tony
gave an insight into his own biography which I don't want
to miss here. He said, "When I was a novice, the Provincial,
Father Casasayas, gave us a talk in which he said, 'Now in
the novitiate you are all very fervent and holy, but then with
the long years and absorbing studies, many lose their fervor
and become remiss in their spiritual life. I'm going to give
you a test for you to find out whether you have kept your
fervor through all these coming years. When, after all your
studies, you are going to come out into the field and go to
meet the Provincial to discuss with him your first appoint-
ment, if you tell him that you want to be sent to the missions
(those were for us the mission stations in the villages, as
opposed to our schools and colleges in the cities), that will
mean that you'll have kept your fervor; and otherwise you
have lost your original spirit.' Those were the Provincial's
words to us, and it is curious that though I forgot everything
else he said, I remembered those words, and when my time
came at the end of my studies, I was ready to measure up to
expectations and pass the test. The Provincial was then Father Mann, and I told him proudly and self-consciously, 'I
want to go to the missions.' I had made it. Father Mann,
however, had other ideas on the subject, and sent me to the
States to study psychology and counseling. When I came
back, the Provincial was Father Correia Afonso, who told

me before I could have my say, 'I see in the Provincial's files that you had originally requested to be sent to the missions. I need a man of your type in a mission station, and I am sending you there.' I resented that. It was for me to utter the all-important words about asking to be sent to the missions, not for him to tell me to go. I felt cheated of my moment of glory. Still, I went there . . . and I disliked the job cordially. Then I took my own vengeance. I started a campaign proclaiming loudly that more Indian fathers should be sent to mission stations, which till then had been mostly manned by Spanish Jesuits. Since I had been manipulated into going to a mission station, I wanted now others like myself to go the same way. I was doing to others what I, unwittingly, had done to myself. That is what we always do."

Another insight into the place of love in his life. The year I was in De Nobili College, Poona, for my long Sadhana, on August 15, feast of the Assumption of Our Lady and India's Independence Day, Tony presided at the concelebrated Eucharist for the whole student body and preached a beautiful homily which many will remember as I do, and whose central idea was this: "If I had been asked in the first years of my spiritual endeavor what I wanted people to say in appreciation of me, I would have answered, 'Let them say, He is a holy man.' Years later I would have answered, 'Let them say, He is a loving man.' And now I would like people to say of me, 'He is a free man.'" He told me later that day that he had prepared the homily carefully, and had even rehearsed it with a younger friend to clarify his ideas and ensure pointed delivery. The progression of values from holiness through love to freedom can stand as a fair summary of clear stages in his life. There still remained the final Lonavla stage, and I wonder what label he would have chosen for it. It certainly was a new and different stage.

He also said, "Love is absence of fear," in Joannine echo, "Perfect love casts out fear." And, "Love is sensitivity to reality." He explained this last saying with the case of a woman in Sadhana who felt attracted to a man in the group and asked him for his friendship. He, politely, told her that he already had a special woman friend in the group and did not want to have another. She felt rejected and cried over it. But then when she came back to the group she had a new experience: She realized that all in the group were attractive and lovable, a thing which she had not noticed before. Excessive concentration on one person had made her blind to the beauty of all the others.

Perhaps the most important thing Tony said about love, and the possible key to the apparent contradictions I have reflected here (Tony liked to say that truth lies in the coincidence of opposites), was that true love is only possible when there is no attachment. That itself is good for a paradox, and will need the context of the next chapter for its clarification.

The Lotus and the Water

"The world is full of sorrow. The root of sorrow is attachment. The remedy is the dropping of all attachments." That was not the Buddha speaking, but Tony de Mello. He knew Buddhism well, and used its positive points effectively in his books and in his courses. When, after Lonavla, a friend asked me, "What did Tony give you in Lonavla?" I joked, "A course on Buddhism!" I was exaggerating, of course, but there was a point in my narrow summary. He freely used Buddhist stories and quotations to clarify an issue or drive home an argument. In doing that he was only complying with the injunction of Vatican II "to recognize, accept and propagate the true spiritual values of other religions." What many people did not notice was the subtle changes he introduced in the sources he quoted. The words I have just given are a good example. The Buddha is usually reported as having said, "The world is full of sorrow. The root of sorrow is desire. The remedy is the uprooting of desire."

Tony changed "uprooting" to "dropping," and "desire" to "attachment." The first substitution will be appreciated at once by those who remember the previous chapter on change. We don't achieve any spiritual result by forcibly "uprooting" things, but by letting them ripen and "drop" at their own time. The second substitution is even more important. If we are to get rid of all "desire" we are going to become neutral, passive, inert. A person without desires is not a human person, and to avoid suffering by suppressing all desires is like curing a headache by cutting off one's head. Effective, but rather too radical. In fact I believe that such was not the Buddha's intention, and that the word he used (*trishana,* or thirst, eagerness, inordinate desire) has been misinterpreted and mistranslated. Tony simply replaced it by "attachment," and then based his essential approach to peace and happiness on it.

Desire as preference is perfectly acceptable and even necessary for human life. I know my preferences and can exercise them within healthy limits to define my character and direct my life. It is desire as attachment that becomes the greatest obstacle to happiness. Attachment means "I cannot do without it," or, in the case of human relations, "I cannot do without you." That induces dependence, craving, clinging, fear of losing, and anxiety to possess. An infallible way to lose one's peace of soul forever. Tony repeated again and again, "The only cause of suffering (apart from physical pain) is attachment. Drop your attachment, and you will find peace."

Happiness is not the fulfillment of desire. Fulfilling the desire does not liberate from it, but creates a new desire for its repetition. The cycle repeats itself, the need for greater gratification increases each time, as all earthly pleasures are subject to the law of diminishing returns, and frustration sets in. The cycle has to be broken, that is, the attachment has to be dropped. Learn to enjoy things in freedom: If I have it, it's fine, and if I don't have it, it's equally fine. The way to enjoy everything is to stick to nothing.

Tony coined a word: "Happiness is *enoughness.*" The secret is to be content with what comes our way, rejecting nothing and hankering for nothing. The great virtue of contentedness. The attitude of St. Paul as he described it himself to the Philippians: "I know how to have a good meal, and I know how to go hungry." This again is faith in Providence, acceptance of God's will, and friendliness with creation. To take things as they are and to imitate the birds in the sky and the lilies of the field. To take what comes, and to let go what goes. God gave and God took away. Blessed be his name forever!

If the archer shoots to get a price in a competition, his muscles will be stiff, his heart will flutter, and his hand will falter. If he shoots for fun, the bow will feel light and the arrow will fly straight to the target. Attachment to the prize ruins the game. Attachment to life ruins life itself.

Tony was fond of quoting a verse of the Gita: "Plunge into the thick of battle . . . , keeping your heart at the lotus feet of the Lord." The battle of the Bhagavad Gita was no ordinary battle. As Arjuna the warrior surveys the battlefield he sees his own relatives standing among the enemy ranks. His own cousins and uncles are facing him, weapons in hand, ready for the battle to the death. How can he fight his own flesh and blood? How can he kill his brothers? How can he drive into the senseless massacre? He loses heart, puts down his mighty bow, and refuses to fight. Then Shri Krishna, Lord and charioteer (meaningful image of God driving the chariot where man stands to fight the battle of life), reminds him of his duty as a warrior, of the impartial reality of life and death, of the generosity to act without looking at the result of one's actions, and leads him to the harshest of actions with the loftiest of detachments. The

thick of battle . . . and the lotus feet of the Lord. The lotus
in India stands for beauty, symmetry, whiteness, and particularly for its ability, both real and mythical, to stand in the
midst of the waters without itself getting wet. This fact of
nature is linguistically expressed in a compound word which
all Indian languages treasure. In Sanskrit the word *jal* (water) rhymes with *kamal* (lotus), and the expression *jal-kamal*
is the standard summary and repeated reminder in all religious books and all religious preaching of that essential attitude of detachment in the midst of the waters of life. Poeti-
cal expression of what we ourselves mean by our also
standard phrase "to be *in* the world, but not *of* the world."
Thus the lotus is the symbol of detachment, and when
joined adjectivally to the sacred feet of the Lord it empha-
sizes poetically the supreme truth of total detachment as
experienced by the soul in intimate communion with the
Lord. Peace of heart in the midst of the battle of life. No
wonder Tony was so fond of that verse.

He was also very fond of a Japanese proverb which he
repeated to us almost every day, always saying it slowly,
with a pause in the middle, and with a knowing expression
in his face as though to tell us that if we got the point there
was nothing more to get. The proverb was, "If you understand them, things are what they are; and if you do not
understand them . . . [pause] . . . things are what they
are." Don't fret about things. Things are what they are, and
life is what it is, whatever your ideas about it may be. If you
rebel and protest, you are the loser. You are "kicking
against the goad," you are hitting your head against a wall,
you are hurting yourself with the hard rock of reality. But if
you understand and accept reality as it is, you get in tune
with life, you enter the current, you ride the storm, you are
at peace with the world and therefore with yourself.

Here the key word was "understanding." When we

asked Tony, "We agree that it is our attachments that hinder
our progress and we want to get rid of them; but how to do
it?" he answered, "By understanding. You never get rid of
an attachment through effort, through willpower, through
manful resolutions or heroic sacrifices. That never works.
The way to drop an attachment is to see it as an attachment,
to realize what it is, to understand it. Don't oppose it as a
personal enemy, simply drop it as a dead weight. When you
come to know that the stone you treasured as a jewel is a
valueless pebble, you spontaneously throw it away. Open
your eyes and see. Be kind to your own attachments and
you will see their importance diminish; if you fight them,
they will grow and become stronger. Be light about them.
Understand them. And then watch them drop away . . . at
their own time."

His favorite story: A monk in his travels once found a
precious stone and kept it. One day he met a traveler, and
when the monk opened his bag to share his provisions with
him, the traveler saw the jewel and asked the monk to give
it to him. The monk did so readily. The traveler departed
overjoyed with the unexpected gift of the precious stone
that was enough to give him wealth and security for the rest
of his life. However, a few days later he came back in search
of the monk, found him, gave him back the stone, and en-
treated him, "Now give me something much more precious
than this stone, valuable as it is. Give me that which enabled
you to give it to me."

This, of course, is something which cannot be given or
taken, not even defined or grasped. It is something to be
learned, accepted, understood. It is the eye of faith which
sees through the apparent value of things and discovers
their intrinsic worthlessness. Paul's realization that the
things he first valued were mere dung. When that happens,
detachment follows by itself. Tony could be quite classical

here, and appeal, in the best tradition of preachers of all time, to the fact of death and the light it throws on the perishable nature of all earthly things. He would repeat, "Listen from your skeleton," and dramatized the gesture in this way: "I am lying down in my sealed coffin, bones alone, months after my death. Somebody knocks on the lid. Knock, knock. 'Tony, are you there?' 'Yes, sure.' 'Do you know what they are saying about you now up here on earth? They are putting you to pieces and saying all sort of wrong things about you.' 'Oh, what do I care? Leave me alone, please. It's quite peaceful and nice inside here. Don't disturb me.' Once I am listening from my skeleton, praise or insult do not affect me anymore; neither does anything else. All attachments have dropped out from my happy bones. Be friendly with your skeleton and you will acquire wisdom."

Another of Tony's illustrations. The surgeon. He called it the perfect example. The surgeon applies all his skill, powers, and interest to the operation he is performing, but is at the same time without any emotion, bias, or attachment that would precisely impair his work. Do your duty and keep your calm. That attitude saves lives.

No attachment and no rejection. To let things come, and to let things go. To let the water flow and the wind blow. To let the melody sound unhindered. Tony was a lover of music and spoke about it with feeling. "A classical symphony. The perfect experience. A symphony has no purpose, no meaning. There is also no clinging to it and no hastening it. One does not wait till the end to enjoy it, but takes in every note, every chord as it comes and lets it go to welcome the next in uninterrupted flow. Any attempt to stop the performance, any 'attachment' to a single note, will ruin the symphony. Do you know the story of Mulla Nasruddin? He was once playing the violin in the public square, and people gathered round him to hear him. Now, he kept playing just a single note, one and the same, all the time. People stopped him and asked him, 'Why do you play the same note the whole time on your violin? See those other street musicians, they all play a variety of notes and a variety of tunes and melodies on their violins, and that is much more entertaining.' The Mulla answered, 'The poor fools! They are all still searching for the perfect note; I've found it!' Would you enjoy such a concert? No wonder people do not enjoy life.''

This insistence on non-attachment may help to clarify Tony's concept of love, as I have announced. For him, paradoxically, one could not love a person so long as he was attached to that person. He even defined love as the dropping of all attachments. It is only when I cease to cling to you, to need you, to possess you that I can begin to love you. The rest was mutual dependence, exigence, and indigence. This is the opposite of love. Love requires freedom, and freedom is lost in the attachment. Tony, with characteristic unselfconsciousness which put people entirely at ease even when he was talking about himself, explained the point by referring to his own experience with his best woman friend, mentioning her by name (she was present in the group) and looking at her: "Formerly when we met I used to be anxious to make the best of the meeting, and felt the need, before we parted, to make sure when and where we would meet again. Now I fully enjoy her company when she comes, but when we part neither of us says a word about the next meeting. Fine if we are together, and fine if we are not. We keep meeting when circumstances so work out, but there is no compulsion, no obligation. The less the attachment, the greater the love." He also referred to a similar experience when his own father died. He had been concerned about him and helping him to spend in the best possible way the last years of his life. He was then quite matter-of-fact at his father's funeral, did not indulge in any mourning, and just felt and expressed the closing of a chapter with gentle and firm finality. No scars in his memory.

"Is it possible to drop all attachments?" somebody asked him. "I don't know," he answered, "but the more we drop, the better."

The Conditioned Brain

"We all carry in our heads a model of reality put there by tradition, training, custom, and prejudice. When the events of life and the behavior of persons around us conform to this model, we are at peace; and when they don't conform, we feel upset. Thus, what in truth upsets us is not those persons or those events, but the model we carry with us. This model is arbitrary and accidental. Realize that, and you will not feel upset anymore at anything."

With that, Tony had said something important which he would repeat day by day till he made it into one of the basic themes of the whole course. My upset does not come from outside reality, but from my inner conditioning. Remove the conditioning and the upset disappears. My way of thinking and of looking at things, my principles and judgments, even my tastes and preferences are the result of the long process which has been my living in a particular family-school-church-society framework. That framework has shaped my mind and channeled my thought, and has determined how I must react "spontaneously" (that is, with "hereditary spontaneity"!) to facts and situations. That can be very useful and even necessary, but it also imposes at times views and outlooks which are not necessary, and which I keep on dragging along in my life allowing myself to be ruled by them. I feel happy when those acquired habits order me to be happy, and feel miserable when according to them I must feel miserable. This sensation does not come from an objective reality, but from an inner bent, and therefore I can now change it if I judge it convenient for my own good and the good of others. To recognize that my upsets come from myself is the first step to remedying them.

Tony set about proving his point: "Something that upsets you may not upset another person. This shows that the cause of the upset was not any objective reality but your own perception of it. If the cause had been outside, it would have affected the other man too; but the fact that it has not proves that the cause was inside you. The model in your head was different from the model in the other man's head, and so you were affected by the incident, while the other man was not. A married man in India would be upset if he invited a guest to his house and the guest would sleep with his (the host's) wife. An Eskimo, apparently, is not upset if his guest behaves in that way, and may in fact invite him to do so. The two married men have different mental models of what is proper, and so react differently. The outside fact is the same, but the inner perception differs. Change your perception and you will change your reaction. The point of the example is that you must not blame your inner upset on outside causes. It comes from inside. From your conditioned brain."

A diamond looks precious to us, but is regarded as valueless by some African tribes. We recoil at dirt while children enjoy playing with it. It all depends on the picture created in the brain. The model, the conditioning, the programming. The great conclusion is that all suffering (again, apart from physical pain) does not come from objective causes but from my inner programming. My brain has been programmed to enjoy certain things and resent others, and it follows blindly the program. When I find myself resenting something, chafing at something, disturbed by something, I have only to change the program and the disturbance will cease.

Tony reached this conclusion in two stages corresponding to Sadhana I and Sadhana II, and I shall set them out separately. Already in Sadhana I Tony had insisted with repeated vehemence, "Nobody upsets you; you upset yourself." In that he was merciless. People complained, "So-and-so annoys me, upsets me, gets on my nerves"; but he never admitted such complaints. "Since when have you given him or her permission to annoy you, to upset you, to get on your nerves? Since when have you surrendered to another person the power over your life? You have given to someone else the key to your freedom and your life, and now you are amused when he amuses you, and are annoyed when he annoys you. What kind of person are you, then?" Tony showed no pity on such defaulters. To blame one's own troubles on someone else was only an escape, a defense mechanism, a shifting of the responsibility from my own head to that of the others, a making myself into a helpless victim who could do nothing except patiently bear the suffering that others were inflicting upon me. This cowardly attitude was ruthlessly denounced, unmasked, and rejected.

Typical examples: "He has insulted me, he has ignored me, he has cheated me, he has harmed me." Typical answer: "If there are any steps to be taken to counteract whatever harm he has plotted against you, take them and settle the matter man to man; but what will never do is to sit idle in your misery, complain to the four winds of the injustice meted out to you, and pretend that we sympathize with you and side with you. By no means. If you want to suffer, suffer by all means, but shoulder the responsibility for your suffering and recognize that it comes from yourself, from your anger at your impotence and cowardice, from your self-rejection, from your defeat without a fight, and from your ensuing frustration. You are harassing yourself; no one else does.

Tony enjoyed acting out the following scene. He is standing in a line, waiting impatiently for his turn, when someone comes up from behind, jumps the line, and gets ahead of him. Then Tony starts crying, takes any handy object to whack himself with (not a hard one so as not to hurt himself), and starts hitting himself on the head while he cringes and wails, "See that man . . . he is hurting me . . . he is unfair to me . . . he has got ahead of me and has no right to do so; poor me, how much I have to suffer!" Lesson: If a man jumps the line, tell him civilly and invite him to take his place; if he listens to reason and goes back, you have won your point, and if he threatens violence you simply reason out that it is preferable for you to wait one more turn than to suffer physical harm, and remain contentedly where you are. But in no case take refuge in the "he is harassing me" and make yourself miserable under the excuse that someone else is doing it. This is a very common game, responsible for much of the misery in this world.

Tony had always said and emphasized that. But now in Sadhana II he went one step further. In Sadhana I he had said, "It is not the other person that harasses you, it is yourself." Now in Sadhana II he sharpened his thought a little more: "It is not you that are harassing yourself, your programmed brain does it." That is, I am not consciously finding excuses and blaming others for my sufferings, it is only my programmed brain that makes me do that, the model that history and tradition have shaped and fixed and fitted into my mind that makes me think that way and act in that manner. I have been taught that if I don't achieve success I must feel bad, if I am not loved I must sulk, if I make a mistake I must feel sorry, if a friend dies I must mourn. And I feel bad and sorry and sulk and mourn accordingly, and bend my head dutifully under unending sufferings as I have been taught to do, and believe to be my sacred duty to do.

There is no such thing. There is no such sacred duty. There is only a prefabricated structure within my brain that forces me now to feel good in certain occasions and bad in others in a wholly arbitrary way. That structure determines my happiness or my misery the way the wind blows. I am a slave to my conditioning.

Tony: "I have been taught to believe that I cannot be happy without money. That is an illusion. Drop the illusion and you'll be happy without money, as many people indeed are. I now feel strongly that I could not be happy without freedom. Yet when I was in my novitiate I had practically no freedom and was very happy indeed. I began to feel unhappy only when I was told that I could not be happy without freedom, and then I felt almost ashamed that I had been without freedom for a period of my life. We need human company because we have been conditioned to believe so. In fact friendship is not necessary for happiness; it may help for growth, but need not give happiness. I feel guilty if I don't achieve a regular devotional prayer life, because that has been hammered into me since my tender religious years; but in fact God is above my prayer habits and I can have a very satisfactory relationship with him even if my prayer life is not a model. How much guilt, resentment, self-hatred, frustration, and suffering come from the image that has been engraved in my mind and the tyrannical injunction to conform to that image! If only I can get rid of that, my life will be happy, satisfied, and peaceful to a much higher degree than it is now."

The password now was, "Drop the illusions." The illusion that you need this person, this thing, this result, this event, this circumstance, this reaction, this security, this certainty in order to be happy. These are only illusions created in the mind by indoctrination and habit. The well-meant brainwashing to which we have been submitted from childhood for our own good, and which has instead caused our ruin. Drop the illusions. Nothing is necessary. Once you break free from the internal compulsion that had made you believe those things were necessary, you will be surprised to find how easily you can live without them. These "illusions" are in fact nothing else than another name for the "attachments" we have been dealing with so far. Both mean "that without which I have been led to believe I cannot do." Both are workings of the mind. And both can be got rid of only by the inner realization of what they are. See, open your eyes, understand. The moment you see an illusion for the illusion it is, it'll drop out by itself. There is no other way. No logic, no argument, no exercise, no force. Just watch the workings of your mind and realize that all your suffering comes from your programmed brain. Seeing the illusion as illusion is dropping it. The tape in your computer has been changed. One suffering less in your life. Keep watching your illusions and changing your tapes. Keep clearing from your brain all the rust and dirt it has accumulated through the years, and health and happiness will return to your life.

A Japanese saying: "The noise does not disturb you; you disturb the noise." Its meaning: "I am annoyed because someone is making a hell of a noise nearby, and I cannot concentrate on my work, cannot study, cannot sleep. The noise is disturbing me. I get impatient and angry, I curse the noise and those who are making it, but I cannot stop them as they are workers doing a repairing job and they have full right and obligation to be where they are and to do what they are doing, which involves a great deal of noise. Still, I am disturbed and grow more and more furious with them and with myself. Yes, with myself, because I know there are people working and living where I am, who are not at all disturbed by the noise. They can work and sleep through an earthquake, while the flight of a mosquito is enough to upset me. Why should I be that way? How can the others be so calm? When the hell is that noise going to stop? Is my head going to explode, or shall I get out of here before I burst? Pretty plight I'm in." One thing is plain: It is not the noise that is disturbing me, because other people in this house are hearing the same noise and are not disturbed. So what is disturbing me is not the power driller but my curled-up nerves. One step further: What do I mean by "my curled-up nerves"? That is simply the principle imprinted in my brain cells from my youth that I am a very sensitive person, that I need quiet and privacy for my work, that I cannot stand noise, that in a civilized environment there should be no noise, and that I am entitled under the UN charter of human rights to lead a noiseless existence free from decibels and from power drillers in the neighborhood of my delicate ears. All that, of course, is trash and rubbish. I have been conditioned to reject noise, just as other persons have been conditioned to tolerate it, and others even to like it and not to be able to live without it; I know such cases too. And now the great defense: "Yes, I admit, I have been conditioned that way, and that is why I now find noise intolerable; I myself wish now that it were not so, but, well, once the harm is done, it's done. My nerves are now that way, and it is too late in life to change them. All that is left for me is to suffer without hope of relief, to stop my ears, to lose my sleep, to be handicapped forever for my oversensitivity to noise, to resign myself to my fate." This defense has to be pulled down immediately if I am to grow. It is true that I have been conditioned to feel that way, but once I know it, all I have to do to remedy the situation is to change the conditioning. To change the tape in the computer. Or, rather, to free the computer from the tape, and the mind from the conditioning. It is never too late to drop the artificial outlook that has been imposed on me, and go back to nature, to reality as it is. Then I will realize that far from the noise disturbing me, "I disturb the noise." That noise, whether it comes from the unavoidable hammering of dutiful workers or from the irresponsible exhaust pipe of a motorcycle without silencer, is part of the reality that surrounds me. That reality is there, for good or for evil, and if I reject it because it does not fit with my wishes and needs, it is I who am disturbing that reality and the noise in it. Resisting reality is, again, "kicking against the goad," and the only person to be harmed is myself. If I learn to change my outlook, to reconcile myself to the facts I cannot change, to accept the noise, I will be able to concentrate on my work and to obtain sleep. Japanese wisdom again.

"I repeat," Tony insisted without end, "all your suffering comes from your programmed brain. Don't blame anybody for it, and don't blame yourselves. It is only the machinery inside you that has been wrongly set and has to be gently reset. Keep watching it. Unmask your illusions. Question everything. Do your homework. Nobody can do that for you, and nobody wants to do that for himself. That is why suffering continues. It is hard work, because it involves reflection, introspection, time, and courage. And, chiefly, perseverance. It is not the work of one day. One illusion has to drop after another, and our private storehouse is so full of them that it may take long to clear it altogether. But, here again, the more illusions you drop, the better. Get down to work on yourselves."

One thing I want to say of Tony, and it has its place here: He did work hard on himself. I don't mean here only his preparing his talks, collecting stories, writing his books (I am a writer, and I know what a hard job it is to write); but his direct work at improving himself, his doing to himself first whatever he later recommended to others, his self-examination, going through exercises, getting feedback, trying experiments, forever thinking, checking, exploring. I could see him sitting alone, sometimes for hours, on the terrace of the new building in Lonavla, and I knew he was not precisely daydreaming. He was planning, practicing, meditating. One day he told us, "Yesterday I said here that all grief is self-pity. Then one of you told me it need not be so. I thought about it for a long time last night, and I think he is right. There are some cases in which grief need not be self-pity. I correct what I said."

Through the years I knew him I got a few hints of what he did when he went through personal crises, which, as everybody else, he too had to endure. Here they are. "When I get lost and don't know what to do, I just go blank and pray to Our Lady."—"The other day I became the frightened child, and started walking aimlessly through the garden alone. What saved me then was the 'Jesus prayer' with rhythmical breathing."—"When I feel low, very low, I go for very long walks several hours alone."—"The best way I have found to get out of my crises is to help others to get out of theirs." In one of his books he has told the story of the guru who attained illumination, and was asked by his disciples what difference it made to have reached that ultimate stage. The guru answered, "Before my illumination, I had depressions; after my illumination, I have depressions." Though he knew we all had read his books and knew the stories in them, he repeated to us that story twice in Lonavla. I could not help feeling it had some bearing on himself.

Use Suffering to End Suffering

"Nobody wants to be healed." Tony repeated time and again his indictment in the midst of everybody's protests. We stay with you for nine months, we come year after year for our Renewals, we spare no effort, we generously put ourselves through all the training and work and exercises you devise for us . . . and you still say nobody wants to be healed. Tony stood his ground: "Ask any therapist, any psychiatrist, any counselor, and he will bear me out. It is a well-known fact in their profession that their clients don't go to them to get cured. They only seek to be relieved of their symptoms, to show that they have made an effort by going to consult an expert, to learn themselves some tricks to try on others, or, quite often, to prove that they are beyond remedy and nobody can cure them. Rare is the person who really wants to be healed, wants total liberation, total detachment, total freedom from all conditioning, and is ready to take the trouble and pay the price to attain that state. It is true of this situation also that 'many are called and few are chosen.' Strive to enter through the narrow door!"

Tony was only expressing in modern terms a traditional consideration of his father St. Ignatius who in a classic text had divided religious mankind into three classes, exemplified in three pairs of business partners who had come by a large sum of money "not purely out of love of God" (Ignatius had his own irony too!) and wanted to settle their consciences and "find God in peace." The first pair says that, of course, they want to set things right, and definitely will do so . . . at the hour of death. Ignatian irony again, though not without a touch of realism. The point is simply procrastination. Yes, we surely want to do it, but not right now, tomorrow, later, we shall see. That is, yes but no. The patient wants to be healed, but is not ready for the operation. The second pair goes a little further . . . apparently. They are ready to part, not with the money, but with the attachment they have to the money, and so they keep the capital while they promise to use it wisely and properly. None of these will "find God in peace." Only the third pair is ready to part with everything, to give up the money now and set right their consciences and their relationship with God. These are few. Few people want truly to be healed, and that was all Tony was saying.

He had spoken of attachments, illusions, conditioning. And he repeated that nobody wanted to get rid of them. We are attached to our attachments, charmed by our illusions, and used to our conditioning. We don't easily give them up, even when officially engaged in doing so, as in a Sadhana course. We compromise, temporize, satisfy ourselves with half measures and meager results, when the only way to achieve something worthwhile in the way of liberation is to go at it wholeheartedly without drawing the line or counting the cost. Tony did not miss any opportunity to urge us on to full generosity in our spiritual endeavor. He knew that a liberated person is the greatest blessing to society in whatever field and whatever circumstances, and strove to form such persons, that is, he strove to encourage us to form ourselves as, at the same time, deeply spiritual and psychologically healthy persons.

For that he did set forth the lines of attack. Without any shortcuts, easy tricks, or ready formulas, he defined clearly his general approach to mental health and spiritual depth. He even gave it a name: suffering to end suffering. The idea in itself is simple enough. Pleasure is fine, and makes us have a good time when it comes, but pleasure does not teach us. Suffering does. Suffering always brings a lesson with itself, and if we profit by those lessons as they come in our life, we are on our way to growth and to maturity. The obstacles to our growth—we know them already—are our attachments, illusions, and conditionings. Now, what suffering does is to uncover those hidden obstacles to us. When I find something disturbing, that means that some attachment, illusion, or conditioning of mine has been hit; that is my chance to become aware of it, unmask it, and get rid of it. Thus suffering is the royal way to health.

"Our tragedy [Tony's words] is not what we suffer, but what we miss when we suffer. We miss the opportunity to grow through suffering. We grow more through rejection than through acceptance, because acceptance breeds complacency, while rejection brings awareness of the points in us that need correction. My only guru is the person who disturbs me, because he reveals my problem to me. Rejoice, then, when a negative feeling has been aroused in you, because if you follow it up, it will lead you closer to liberation. All growth occurs through suffering, if only you know how to use suffering to end suffering. Don't distract yourself from the suffering, don't rationalize it, don't justify it, don't forget it, don't neglect it. The only way to deal with suffering is to face it, to observe it, to understand it. What illusion is behind this suffering? What attachment of mine has it inflicted itself upon? What conditioning has it violated? There is my golden chance to know myself, to check my weaknesses, to improve my life. Instead, we blame others for our sufferings, we complain against our rivals, society, the government, and God himself, we escape into self-pity or bitterness or a nervous breakdown or try to drown our depression in hard work or cynical misery. If we only learn how to profit by our sufferings, we will advance fast in our spiritual life."

To put it another way: Every time I suffer, I am resisting reality. Suffering is simply resistance to reality. I had obscured reality by my attachments, illusions, and conditioning, and now reality, when it presents itself to me as it is and as I don't anymore know it, hurts me. The question, then, to ask when suffering comes is, What am I resisting? Not, What is wrong with the world? but, What is wrong with me? Every time I am disturbed, there is something wrong with me. I am not prepared for what has come, I am out of tune with things, I am resisting something. Find out what that is. That will give light and open the way to spiritual advance.

Tony tackled me in the group: "You say you have trouble with your sleep. You blame your nerves, your work, the noise, and the heat. Rather think for a moment: What reality are you avoiding? Knowing you, it is easy for me to say it: You are resisting your not being in control of yourself. You have been trained to rule your own life, to keep your mind and body under strict discipline, to be in charge of yourself. And in this important matter of your daily sleep, you are not. You want to sleep, and you cannot. That situation is intolerable to you. You resent the loss of control, and resist it with all your might. The result is a sleepless night. You also resist the fact that while you are lying in bed without sleep you are 'wasting time.' You are a compulsive worker, and the very idea of lying down idle is repugnant to you. You then try to convert the 'wasted time' into 'useful time' by praying or planning while lying awake. Praying and planning is fine, but as you do that in order to fight the waste of time and to protest against it, it only makes the situation worse. You also compare yourself to other people you know who sleep soundly as soon as they hit the pillow, you feel jealous of them and rebel against the unfairness of it all. You are afraid that lack of sleep will impair your health and your capacity to work, and feel ashamed to think that if you don't get sleep tonight you'll be yawning tomorrow the whole day in front of everybody and you will be embarrassed. No wonder that to avoid all that pain you reach for the sleeping tablet. This gesture is the final expression of your rejection of the situation, and brings in more trouble. The sleeping tablet may give you rest for a night, but it has a much more important and baneful side effect. It reinforces your inner conditioning against the no-sleep situation, and blocks your acceptance of it. You have increased your problem by fighting it. That breeds anxiety: Will I need a tablet again next night? Will I get addicted? How long will this last? Where will it take me? Quite an involved problem, and it all comes from your own conditioning. Your programmed brain forbids you to think that you can be happy so long as you experience sleeplessness, and orders you to remove it. You resist your lack of sleep, and thereby increase it. Don't resist sleeplessness. Don't escape discomfort. Trust your body, which knows perfectly well how much it wants to sleep and when, if you only leave it alone to its own wisdom. I warn you that this is hard to do. Get in touch with your resistance. Watch it. Accept it. Let your nights be whatever they are, and your days be whatever they are. And don't even feel greedy to have your problem solved. You can be happy even if you don't sleep well. Any more questions?"

This may give a taste of what Tony meant by "using suffering to end suffering." That is, welcoming suffering because it brings to our attention our weaknesses, alerts us to our inner needs, urges us to put a remedy to them, and offers us the means to do so by seeing reality as it is, facing it and accepting it. This removes the root of suffering instead of only alleviating symptoms. Another expression for this was "to end suffering by understanding it." Seeing, knowing, realizing. The eye of faith on the realities of life.

Tony again: "Happy experiences make life delightful; painful experiences lead to growth. This does not mean that we are to seek suffering and provoke pain; there is enough suffering in life to add to it on our own. But it does mean that we must use suffering when it comes for this noble purpose. Don't let the chance pass. Never say, 'When this suffering passes, I'll be happy again.' No. If you are not happy with things as they are with you now, you'll never be. If you wait to be out of jail in order to be free, you'll never be free. Learn how to be and feel free while you are in jail, and then you can be free anywhere."

Innocent and Blameless

"Never see people as good or bad, but think always of all men and women as totally selfish, greedy, vicious, stupid, innocent, and blameless." If Tony said those words once in Lonavla, he said them ten times. Behind them was one of his pet ideas, closely related to the conditioning I have just explained. The idea is that people act always the best way they can in the circumstances, and so they are in any case innocent and blameless; but their lifelong conditioning leads them to think "best" something which to us, with a different conditioning ourselves, seems at times stupid or vicious. This is not denying the existence of free will in the acts of man, but only emphasizing the role played in them by their previous conditioning, so as to pave the way for a better understanding of the way other people behave, and to reduce the gap between "the good guy" and "the bad guy" which we all have inherited from the motion pictures and carry with us, with unfortunate consequences, into our dealings with others. One of Tony's books carries the story that if good people were white and bad people black . . . little Mary Jane would be streaky! That is the point.

We are morally responsible for our actions, we are accountable to our conscience, to society, and to God, and we need God's pardon when we, knowingly and willingly, depart from the path of his commandments. Together with this, the realization that at times we are not as free as we thought we were can help us to be kind when judging ourselves, and still more when judging others.

It is a fact of Christian tradition that saints sincerely see themselves as the worst of sinners. This is not exaggerated humility or veiled hypocrisy, but the plain and sincere recognition of all they know to be inside them, which they see more clearly by the light of grace in which they abound. That dark side of their beings is kept down in their lives by the mercy of God, but they know it, and when they see it come to the surface in others they recognize at once their kinship with all that is worst in the world. A Sufi saying expounds the same idea from another angle: "A saint is a saint till the moment he knows he is a saint." We all, when hearing news of people who have fallen (and whom we are already judging!) have felt sharply in our lives that other saying: "There but for the grace of God go I!" St. Augustine knew by experience in the first part of his life what it was to yield to temptation, and he also knew that after his conversion and consecration he was the same he had always been, capable again to be unfaithful as he was now to be generous, and expressed his feeling poignantly while recording the fidelity of the second part of his life with the same sincerity with which he had recorded his infidelity in the first: *"Domine, ut occasio deesset tu fecisti!"* ("It was you, Lord, who removed the occasion!") If the occasion had come again, the fall also would have followed, because the person that had fallen was the same. When the circum-

stances changed, the behavior changed. There is no boast
and no condemnation. Even when some people seem to us
to act wickedly, they do not act out of malice, but out of
ignorance. Here Tony had the whole backing of Scripture.
"They will kill you thinking they are doing a service to
God"; "They do not know what they are doing"; "I am the
worst of sinners . . . , but I acted in ignorance" (Paul);
and the "unwitting sins" (unknown to the sinner) of Psalm
18.

Tony told us about a little exercise he carried out with a
group of religious people. He told them to take paper and
pencil and write down, without giving their names, five acts
they could remember in which they had acted out of malice
in their lives. All the papers came back blank. Nobody,
when confronted honestly with his own conscience without
fear of rejection and without false humility or the need to
hide anything, could say that he had truly acted anytime out
of malice. True, those were religious people, but if the experiment were conducted among a group of people socially
regarded as wrongdoers, the papers would come back blank
again. Nobody acts out of sheer personal malice. Even the
terrorist, while placing a bomb which will kill innocent people, believes he is doing his duty, sometimes at great risk to
himself, he is working for his group or for his country, or
even "doing a service to God." "Do not judge," insisted
Jesus to his disciples . . . to little effect.

The difference between the act of the terrorist as terrorist
and the act of the social worker as social worker is that the
act of the social worker is beneficial to society, while the act
of the terrorist is harmful to it, and so society exalts one and
condemns the other. Society does well to reward those who
help it and repress those who harm it. Where society goes
wrong, and all of us with it, is in extending its judgment
from the act (helpful, harmful) to the person (good, bad),
and judging motives and intentions from the acceptability

or nonacceptability to itself of the results or consequences of those actions. "Condemn the sin, but not the sinner" is the old principle which acquires new relevance today.

Imputation of motives is so common with us that we claim to know why people act the way they act, when very often those people themselves don't quite know their own true motives. "He has done it again; of course he would. He is acting out his own needs and wants to make people dependent on him to prop his own insecurity. Everybody sees that. It is so obvious. And then, of course, he goes and tells everybody he is doing that for the good of the others. That's a good joke! The trouble with the poor man is that he has told that story so often that he believes it now himself! He believes his motives to be entirely altruistic when in fact they are absolutely selfish. The man is truly to be pitied."

What is truly pitiful is such a comment, though unfortunately it is not so rare with us. To learn to respect other people's consciences is Christian charisma and human elegance.

Another angle from which Tony focused the same question was the following. All damage to others is eventually damage to oneself, and we know this in our heart of hearts. Maybe passion blinds us at the moment of acting, and we find ourselves hurting others with mad violence; but we know all the time that those blows will eventually turn on ourselves, and making others suffer will make us too suffer in the long run. He who kills by the sword dies by the sword. Hurting my neighbor is, sooner or later, in one way or another, hurting myself. Since nobody, then, acts willfully to damage himself, nobody acts for the sake of damaging others either. That is, nobody acts out of malice, even when the external result of his action makes it appear so. The real motive of acting, hidden perhaps to the external observer but evident to him who acts, is, in the last analysis, to do what the person thinks is most beneficial for himself in the circumstances, given his own outlook, training, and conditioning; and this includes (maybe also "in the last analysis," and passing first through the terrorist's bomb) doing what in his understanding is going to be more beneficial for all. Nobody hits another for the sake of hitting, unless he is insane. Every member of a group (even when that group is the human race) knows that his own welfare depends on the welfare of the group, and that is the ultimate end of all his efforts, however misguided. Nobody knowingly cuts the branch of the tree on which he is sitting. The effects of one's action may be wild and strange, because the human mind does wild and strange things, but the original motive of all actions is self-preservation, which includes the necessary preservation of the others too. When man hurts man it is blind passion rather than refined malice that moves his hand.

In the normal course of life we, inevitably, have to evaluate and pass judgment on actions and attitudes that affect us, but even then we must carefully distinguish between the practical judgment of what this person and his actions mean for me now and the moral judgment of what he is in himself. I can rate the performance of people in the same way and with the same detachment and objectivity with which I rate the performance of a secretary or a travel agent (these are Tony's examples): This agent does a good job, is punctual, efficient, reliable; or, on the contrary, is useless, inefficient, and lazy. This is a practical appraisal of a person's work, which will influence my dealings with that person, my engaging that travel agent or another; but without, in any case, judging the person as such. We never judge the person. Jesus did not condemn the adulterous woman.

An important consequence of this is that when people around us act in ways which we find obnoxious or offensive to us, we have no grounds to protest or complain against the persons who act in that way. We'll do well, to be sure, to protect ourselves from the harm that might result to us from their actions, but, again, we have no quarrel with the persons as such. I could protest if my "enemy" acted out of malice against me, but in fact he is doing nothing of the kind; he is just protecting his own interests, promoting himself, doing what he believes to be the best for himself or even for society—in a word, being "totally selfish, greedy, vicious, stupid, innocent, and blameless." I can only leave him alone. Let me learn never to blame people.

Another consequence: There is nothing to forgive between man and man. All apologies, pardons, and explanations among us are meaningless. Nobody has offended me, in the first place, so why should I ask for an apology? Whatever he has done to me, he has done it thinking that was what he should be doing; then how can I ask him to take back his words or make amends for his act? To ask for forgiveness, and even to grant it, is to recognize that there was guilt, evil, and malice; once we recognize that such is not the case, there is no place left for forgiveness. Forgiveness serves only to emphasize discord. (How true!, I thought while listening to Tony. Once in my life I was asked to apologize to a professor for not attending his classes. I dutifully did so, he graciously forgave me . . . and from that moment, to this day, we hated each other cordially.) Pardon does not exist because the offense does not exist; and the offense does not exist because the intention does not exist. True forgiveness is only the realization that there is nothing to forgive.

Here comes an important point which Tony elucidated with firm clarity when someone, inevitably, brought up the question. We have said that people who act in an unpleasant or harmful way against others do so because of their conditioning, the totality of their habits, prejudices, and beliefs which lead them to see things in a particular way and react accordingly. And, of course, the same is true of people who act in a pleasant and helpful way toward others: They do so because of their inherited and acquired way of looking at things and events and reacting to them. Could we, then, say that there is a "bad conditioning" that leads people to act badly and a "good conditioning" that leads them to act well? No. All conditioning is bad in itself. The result of a conditioning to do things pleasant to us is agreeable to us, just as the conditioning to do unpleasant things is disagreeable; but the conditioning as such, the bending of the mind, the inducing of prejudice, the screening, the censoring, the brainwashing (whether with a good or with a bad intention) is always to be rejected. It goes against the dignity of the person, the freedom of the mind, and the ultimate health of the individual and of society. To drop all conditionings (or, again, as many as we can) is the way to inner peace and universal concord.

It is important to realize that behind that attitude there is a fundamental trust in human nature and in God who created it. This religious optimism permits us to trust in the human person, to accept his instincts and defend his integrity against any attempt at mental subjugation, wherever it may come from. Man is better than he is taught to be. True, there is original sin and human concupiscence in the heart of man; but there is also, and more abundantly, the grace of God and the divine sonship of all his children. Faith in man is faith in God.

I want to emphasize how much this teaching fits in with Tony's general outlook on man and life and God. No need to forgive, no judging, no blaming . . . it is part of that general attitude to nature and to all things in it that leads us to accept things as they are, to welcome reality, to realize that nobody hurts me, that people need not change, that I am fine as I am, and that faith and trust are the basis of a happy life rather than protest and rebellion. Avoiding misunderstandings and speaking of the person in his attitude toward himself (not of social revolution which history may justify and require), the personal integration of all one is and lives, including the most painful aspects of being, is the clear and firm direction along which lie the growth and fullness of the human person.

This is the everlasting meaning of Jesus' original and unconditional commandment: "Do not resist evil." For all our humble limitations in understanding all the meaning Jesus put in those words, and for all the controversy it raises in our hearts when we want to carry it into practice and to reconcile it with our deepest duty to fight injustice and oppose oppression, that commandment points to a peace of soul and an equanimity of mind which are our evangelical heritage, and are to accompany us wherever we go and whatever we do, in order to make our action fruitful and our presence beneficent. "Do not judge," "do not resist," "nor do I condemn you," "go in peace." Divine blessing on man's humble heart.

Good Luck? Bad Luck?

Declaring all people innocent and blameless did not free Tony from the task of answering innumerable questions on moral problems and human behavior. He plunged cheerfully into the task, since he realized perfectly well that in order to form a person he had to form his or her conscience, a conscience which, only too often, reached his hands after it had been deformed by rigors, scruples, fears, and prejudices. All that had to be purified so that the soul's psychological peace could become the basis and condition of its spiritual peace. An important mission which Tony carried out with great firmness on one side, and great sensitivity on the other, always alert to what the given person at the given moment needed and could bear. He was aware of his responsibility as arbiter of consciences, with an authority whose weight he felt in the midst of all the jokes and laughter that enlivened his interventions.

His first condition was to deal with the present moment and with the person in front of him. No hypothesis, no conjectures, no artificial situations or abstract possibilities. The here and now. The person and his case. Questions like, "What would you do if . . . ?" or "What would you advise to a person who . . . ?" were disallowed. If the problem is yours, and you have the courage and trust to speak in the first person in the middle of the group, do so; and if for any reason you don't want that, role-play, that is, speak here and now as though you were the person who has the problem and wants an answer, and think and react as you imagine he would do it. The exchange has to be person-to-person and in the present tense. This is not a chair in a divinity school, but a training for life, and so the problems and the way to present and tackle them have to be active and vivid. The best approach to understanding and solving a problem is to live it.

The second condition Tony imposed with definite rigor on anyone who consulted him was that the responsibility to decide and choose a final way of action (or to reject all of them, which also was possible) fell squarely on the client. Nobody will tell you what you have to do, nobody will take in your name the decisions that you alone have to take. There will be feedback, advice, sounding boards, reactions of all kinds, even theory and doctrine when necessary, but the final responsibility can never be delegated. Here came into full play the "client-centered therapy" which gently returns the questions to the client, mirrors and echoes his feelings to help him clarify his own standing till he finds a way out by himself. This does not mean that Tony would limit himself to a passive role when directing others (it is impossible to imagine Tony playing a passive role in anything at all!); he knew how to attack, to corner an escapist, even to insult if that could help to shake up a sluggard, though always with total respect for the person at the moment when the person is more a person, which is when he considers all the options and chooses one. That is the essence of the moral act, and people have to accept in it the awesome and glorious burden of their solitary responsibility. They, in the last analysis, have to run their lives themselves.

After these two conditions came the general principle Tony followed when considering moral options and problems of conscience, which was this simple and practical rule: Don't harm anybody, and help those you can. In the complex world of all rules and principles of human behavior, the firm and brief summary "Don't harm anyone" brings with itself a great light, peace, and strength which simplify life and rationalize behavior with a touch of common sense and a whiff of fresh air. This brief summary is enough to clarify most decisions, and satisfies most people in the practice of their day-to-day moral life. As a practical guide through the jungle of moral decisions it is certainly useful and helpful; as a theoretical principle, however, it has its difficulties, and Tony was clearly aware of them. We have settled that the point is to avoid harm and promote help, but the theoretical difficulty now is, who now decides what is "harm" and what is "help" for my neighbor in these concrete circumstances? And who am I to do that anyhow? Now, if I cannot decide that, how do I rule my behavior toward him? If I decide what is convenient for my neighbor and what is not, I appoint myself as his judge, which is precisely what we want to avoid. If I want to ask him, well, in the first place on many occasions I'll have no chance to do it, and, even if he tells me, I cannot go by that, as nobody is a good judge in his own case, neither my neighbor in his. And if I have to ask God about it, I go back to the textbooks and the scholars and the opinions and the discussions, which, no doubt, are valid and important for those who have to study them, but remain far and remote from the man in the street at the moment of taking the next step in his wandering through life. A look at this question will bring out new aspects in Tony's way of thinking and acting.

Tony's best-known story is the one he printed at the end of his first book, *Sadhana: A Way to God.* It is best known and least understood. I quote it here.

There is a Chinese story of an old farmer who had an old horse for tilling his fields. One day the horse escaped into the hills and when all the farmer's neighbours sympathized with the old man over his bad luck, the farmer replied, "Bad luck? Good luck? who knows?" A week later the horse returned with a herd of wild horses from the hills and this time the neighbours congratulated the farmer on his good luck. His reply was, "Good luck? Bad luck? Who knows?" Then, when the farmer's son was attempting to tame one of the wild horses, he fell off its back and broke his leg. Everyone thought this very bad luck. Not the farmer, whose only reaction was, "Bad luck? Good luck? Who knows?" Some weeks later the army marched into the village and conscripted every able-bodied youth they found there. When they saw the farmer's son with his broken leg they let him off. Now was that good luck? Bad luck? Who knows? Everything that seems on the surface to be evil may be a good in disguise. And everything that seems good on the surface may really be an evil. So we are wise when we leave it to God to decide what is good luck and what bad, and thank him that all things turn out for good with those who love him.

I had always suspected that in that story there was more than met the eye. Tony was very fond of it, told it often, even to people who surely knew it, as though he wanted them to see deeper into it, and he himself had left the story open-ended with a general reference to the Christian hope that "all manner of things will be well." Apart from this beautiful reassurance and Christian optimism that emanated from the story, as told by Tony, in the midst of a difficult world, I thought that the story had a bearing on his moral

teaching and his way to direct human behavior, and I
wanted to check with him. I did so during a long walk he
and I alone took an evening in Lonavla. When I mentioned
my hunch he at once smiled and said, "Of course, Carlos.
Isn't it evident? The strange thing is that all read the story
and nobody seems to see the point. They just take the point
that God can make good come out of evil, which is very
true and consoling, and which increases their trust in Divine
Providence and their faith in life. That is a very genuine and
very beautiful fruit of the story; but it is by no means its
main point. The main point has to do with our morality and
our behavior. We had first reduced the volumes of our
moral theology to one practical rule: Don't harm anybody.
That was already quite a step, in line with Jesus' attitude
when he reduced the Law and the Prophets to the double
commandment, Love your God and love your neighbor.
The love of God manifests itself in the love to our neighbor,
and this is the practical application of the love to our neigh-
bors: Don't harm them, and, when possible, help them.
That already frees us from trammels of casuistry, scruples of
conscience, and details of legislation. And now comes an
even greater freedom. If the practical rule of my behavior is
to do what is good and not what is bad for my neighbor,
and then I discover that in fact I never know what in reality
is going to be good or bad for him, that gives me a responsible but genuine freedom in my behavior, doesn't it? Maybe
people are afraid of that freedom, and that is why they don't
want to see the point. There is no question of abetting licen-
tiousness; common sense will always prevail and social life
will be upheld. Conscience has to be heeded, and public
morality to be respected. But, to be honest, we just don't
know what is good and what is bad for anybody, and that, in
the midst of our humble limitations, should give us great
peace at the time of making decisions. We are not burdened
now with the responsibility to solve all problems for every-

body and to ensure the universal welfare of mankind. It is for us only, in the honesty of our conscience and within the boundaries of our actions, to approximate results, and God is the one who will change the bad luck into good in his providence. If we only understood this, the burden of our moral conscience would be considerably lightened. That is the point of the apparently simple story. Good luck? Bad luck? Who knows? And if we don't know, why worry? In any case it is good luck for us if we get the message, isn't it?"

We still discussed the story further while we walked at a steady pace along the Lonavla road. I had come to the conclusion that the story was one of those universal stories to be found in almost all literatures. I myself had come across equivalent narratives, with different incidents but the same message, in a Sufi story, a Dervish story, and, of course, an Indian story. I told Tony the Indian story, which is set in one of the classic dialogues between the emperor Akbar (whom a popular democratic feeling makes always get the worst of the exchanges) and his minister Birbal (who with an unexpected turn of his ready wit always turns the story to a happy end), and it runs as follows: One day Akbar and Birbal went hunting in the forest. While shooting with his gun, Akbar broke his thumb and felt great pain. Birbal bandaged the wound and offered the emperor some philosophical consolation: "Majesty, we never know what is good or what is bad for us." The emperor did not take kindly to the advice, went into a rage, and threw his minister into a deserted well. Then he continued alone, making his way through the wild jungle when a group of forest people came upon him, surrounded him, took him captive, and led him to their chief. The tribe was about to offer a human sacrifice, and Akbar would now be the God-sent victim. The chief priest, however, while examining him noticed the bandage on his thumb, and rejected him as the victim had to be without blemish. Akbar realized how right Birbal had been, felt remorse, ran back to the well into which he had thrown him, took him out, and asked his pardon for the harm he had unjustly done to him. Birbal answered, "You need not ask any pardon from me, because you have done me no harm. On the contrary, you have done me a very good turn, you have saved my life. If you had not thrown me into the well and I had continued by your side, those savages would have taken me for their sacrifice and killed me. You see, we never know when something is good or bad for us."

Tony commented, "When all cultures coincide on a point, they surely have something to teach us. And the teaching of this universal story seems to be that we are not to take our lives, our decisions, our failures and our successes, and even our moral blunders or our exalted merits too seriously. Let us do whatever we do with a light heart and a happy mind, and all will turn out well at the end. Good luck? Bad luck? Who knows?"

I then had a surprise for Tony. Shortly before going to Lonavla I had come across a text of St. Augustine's which I was sure he would enjoy, and this was the moment of quoting it to him. The text comes from St. Augustine's commentary on the first letter of St. John, and it says, "Do you wish your friend to live? You do well. Do you wish your enemy to die? You do wrongly. Though maybe the life you wish your friend is useless for him, while the death you desire for your enemy is beneficial to him. We never know whether to go on living is good or bad for anybody." Augustine seems to apply our story to life itself. To live? To die? Good? Bad? Who knows? Tony's comment on hearing the text was, "Bad logic and good theology!" Bad logic, because if we do not know that a course of action is beneficial to a person, why should we be obliged to follow it? But good theology and good common sense, because the consideration that death may be good for my enemy does not certainly allow me to kill him. This is our situation. We don't exactly know what is good or bad for us or for anybody, but keep on doing cheerfully what seems to us most appropriate in each case without a weight on our mind or a worry in our heart. That is the full import of the story of the old Chinese farmer. And that was the practical summary of Tony's approach to human behavior.

The God of Awareness

On the first day of the Lonavla meeting Tony announced that one of the topics he would expressly deal with during those days would be our life of faith and prayer, our concept of God and our relationship with him. The subject was, however, lost in the unpredictable mixture that followed, and I find in my notes only occasional references to it. The fact that he mentioned it specifically the first day shows that he had special interest in dealing with it, and the fact that it was lost in the ensuing jumble is perfectly understandable to anyone who knows what those radically informal sessions were like. Some days, after having prepared and announced his topic, Tony would come to the hall, but before he could open his mouth somebody from the group would put up his or her hand to ask a question . . . and Tony's topic was generously forgotten in favor of an urgent need, the whole session taking a totally unexpected turn. This was sometimes irritating to others, and Tony himself did not always yield to sudden requests, yet the lack of systematization was complete, and accounted in this case, as in quite a few others, for a topic's being clearly announced and innocently forgotten.

Already in his early Sadhana years Tony had mimeographed seven pages under the title "Some Notes on Prayer," which were the seed from which his first book, *Sadhana: A Way to God* sprang later. In those notes, as in the book, he makes a clear distinction between "devotional prayer" and "awareness prayer," and that distinction is essential to understand his religious thought. He applied it also directly to God: the God of devotion and the God of awareness. This distinction is traditional in Hinduism, and helps to clarify different approaches of man to God, respecting all and not rejecting any, but exposing the possibilities open to man for him to avail himself of them according to his inclination and his need at a particular time in his life. The Hindu terminology could be informally translated as "the concrete God" and "the abstract God," both appellations referring, of course, to the same Supreme Being, but each one describing a different aspect of his infinite reality as perceived by the limited understanding of man.

The God of devotion refers to the concept of God most of us are used to, the object of our love and worship, of our prayers and our cult; a God we can talk to, and who himself speaks to us in our hearts; a God whose images we can fashion (the "concrete" God) and, while we know them to be only images, we can be helped by them to concentrate our thoughts on him, enliven our faith, and build up our liturgy. He is a God we can fall in love with, feel constantly at our side, call our friend, our brother, our Father and Creator, and relate to him, with due respect and reverence, as to a friend, a brother, and a lover.

Our main link with the God of devotion is prayer in faith, and Tony was a recognized master in that art. Many people were attracted to him by that outstanding quality of his.

Whatever else he was, he was a master of prayer. He himself mentions in the introduction to *Sadhana: A Way to God* that he was surprised to find many spiritual people who did not know how to pray, and spiritual directors who did not know how to teach them. He, on the contrary, asserts there that "it has always been relatively easy for me to help people to pray." A friend of his and mine put it more forcibly: "Tony could teach a stone to pray." He knew his own charisma, exercised it with generosity, and believed so much in the power of prayer and faith that he even thought seriously for a time, and told us so publicly, of going into the healing ministry in the power of the Spirit.

I see three stages in Tony's ministry (which reflected his own personal development), and this is the place to delimit them. Tony as a spiritual director (the Retreat movement); Tony as therapist (Sadhana I); and Tony as a guru (Sadhana II). The labels are, of course, narrow and the stages overlap, but they do respond to a reality and a progress in Tony's thinking and working. He kept advancing steadily throughout his life with an open mind and a ready heart, always combining the best of what he had learned and experienced in the past with the new ways and ideas which he reviewed in the present and felt free to accept precisely because he was solidly grounded in the old.

His own sincerity and openness led him to realize the difficulties raised by the concept of "the God of devotion," however legitimate and fruitful that concept was in itself. He said meaningly once, using the language of Transactional Analysis, "The problem with considering God as Father is that sooner or later he will turn into a critical parent." The "critical parent" is the negative censor and strict controller we all carry within us to impose his or her "parental injunctions" on us, to threaten, to compel, to punish, and so to tame us into reluctant submission out of fear. That is not what God does, but is certainly the way many believers perceive him to be: the image of an insecure God created by insecure man, a God who is afraid man will forget him, is concerned about his own glory, and so wants to control man through strict regulations and severe punishments. Painful caricature of God's supreme majesty, but not altogether unrealistic in the minds of some of those "who fear the Lord" as the Jews called their proselytes. "A religion of fear could hardly be called the Good News," said Tony.

He insistently spoke of "the unconditional love of God," and often quoted J. B. Phillips, the gifted Bible translator, as saying, "The difference between the Old Testament and the New is that in the Old, God loves the just and punishes the sinner, whereas in the New he loves both." Tony illustrated the point with a touching memory of his own life. "Once," he said, "I told my mother to tease and test her, 'If I would leave the priesthood and marry, what would you feel?' She looked sad and answered, 'I would feel great pain; but your wife would be my daughter.' I feel that is the way God loves me too. No conditions to his love."

This was beautiful and consoling, and we all feel in our hearts that such is the real and eternal truth. At the same time, this fond hope is not easily reconciled, at a purely logical level, with the serious dogmas of the last judgment and the existence of hell, and, in general, with the eternal problem that underlies all systems and all philosophies, namely the problem of the existence of human suffering and moral evil in the world. If God loves man and can do everything, even, according to Christian theology, to establish peace and prosperity in the world respecting human freedom, why doesn't he do it? Tony's answer, as that of all contemplatives in all ages and all climates, was not based on constructing syllogisms, but on understanding better the ways of God, purifying the current concept of God, entering deeper in the darkness of faith along the way of the mystics of all religions, and feeling with a loving and believing heart what goes beyond the limitations of human reason.

Tony was something of an authority in mystical theology and practice, and quoted freely and familiarly St. Theresa of Avila, St. John of the Cross, St. Catherine of Siena, Meister Eckhart, Juliana of Norwich, and *The Cloud of Unknowing*. This last treatise was almost compulsory reading for all of us. I quote from it here:

Indeed, if we may say so reverently, when we are engaged on this work it profits little or nothing to think even of God's kindness or worth, or of our Lady, or of the saints or angels, or of the joys of heaven, if you think thereby by such meditation to strengthen your purpose. In this particular matter it will help not at all. For though it is good to think about the kindness of God, and to love him and praise him for it, it is far better to think about him as he is, and to love and praise him for himself. Therefore I will leave on one side everything I can think, and choose for my love that thing which I cannot think! Why? Because he may well be loved, but not thought. By love he can be caught and held, but by thinking never. Therefore, though it may be good sometimes to think particularly about God's kindness and worth, and though it may be enlightening too, and a part of contemplation, yet in the work now before us it must be put down and covered with a cloud of forgetting. And you are to step over it resolutely and eagerly, with a devout and kindling love, and try to penetrate that darkness above you. Strike that thick cloud of unknowing with the sharp dart of longing love, and on no account whatever think of giving up. Trample on your thought out of love for God; yes, even when such thoughts seem to be holy, and calculated to help you find God . . . , even if they are thoughts of Christ's sacred Passion. The practiced hand must leave all thoughts and put them away deep down in the cloud of forgetting if he is ever to penetrate the cloud of unknowing between him and God.

This stilling of the intellect in the presence of the Divine Majesty leads to "the abstract God," "the God of awareness," or "the God of unknowing," which are all words to express the unexpressible. This silence of the mind is the supreme adoration before God; and the finding him in the constant personal awareness of the world he has created around us and within us is the anonymous prayer which in the secret liturgy of the universe unites us to the source of all being with every breath we take and every word we utter in our daily surrender to life. This, to Tony, was deep spirituality, and to obtain it was directed the whole effort of dropping attachments, illusions, and conditionings, in order to reach, in the existential poverty of created beings, the center of life which is God himself. That was the irreplaceable core of Tony's teaching and training.

In my opinion this is one of the richest services Tony ever rendered the persons he dealt with and the Church he loved, that is, to open the mind and the experience of those who listened to him to new ways of understanding and living the supreme reality that is God. This was his great contribution, his answer to the crisis of faith and obedience which haunts consciences and worries the Church, and whose best solution is the search, within our own tradition, of new ways to understand and feel God, not only saving thus our faith and religiosity, but making them grow to God's glory and our own profit. I have written a whole book *(Sketches of God)* based on that idea which I learned from Tony and which has helped me radically in my life and in my dealing with people who search for God; I know its importance, and acknowledge with joy my debt. The first time someone asked me in spiritual direction, "When I do awareness exercises of contact with myself, my breathing, my senses, the surrounding nature, space, the whole of creation . . . do I pray?" my spontaneous answer (prepared by an experience of many years which came to my lips at the moment) was, "Yes, because if you are in contact with yourself, you are in contact with God." I have always felt proud of that answer, which was not rehearsed or anticipated, but was born virgin in my mind as the ripe fruit of the long experience briefly alluded to here.

The key word to Sadhana was "awareness," and once faith makes us see and feel God in all things (let my brother Jesuits think of the "Contemplation to obtain Love" of our Father Ignatius), these exercises become in the end a sacred awareness of the divine presence in us and in all things, an intimate and committed worship in action of him "in whom we live and move and have our being."

Tony's words: "Sadhana will be useless for you unless you deepen in it your sense of the infinite."

The Self and the Non-Self

This was the greatest bombshell Tony had in store for us. He hinted at it repeatedly, announced at every turn that the final answer to each question had to wait till this essential point was elucidated, took a full day to explain it to his own satisfaction, and referred back to it in the remaining days to tie up all he had said throughout the course in this single knot of supreme importance. He called it the end of Sadhana, the ultimate way to eliminate all attachments, illusions, and conditionings, the traditional quest of all mystics and the highest achievement of all saints. That was, in a word, the all-or-nothing, the now-or-never of our spiritual endeavor and of our existence on earth. Here was Tony the guru revealing his sacred *mantra* (salvation formula) to eager inquirers. The only thing that was missing was to have consulted the astrologer for the auspicious astral moment in which the initiation should take place for full effect. I don't think Tony went to that length. But apart from that he spared no efforts to impress on us the importance of what he was going to say.

What he had to say was in fact very easy to say. The Self is the cause of all our troubles. We have given it undue importance, have made of it the center of the universe as though everything had to turn round us, and since in fact it doesn't, we feel hurt and upset. We'll learn to be happy in the measure in which we learn to devalue the "I." The Self is the villain of the piece. Drop the Self (this was Tony's insistingly repeated formula) and you will be free.

"Jesus then said to his disciples: If anyone wishes to be a follower of mine, he must leave self behind; he must take up his cross and come with me. Whoever cares for his own safety is lost; but if a man will let himself be lost for my sake, he will find his true self. What will a man gain by winning the whole world, at the cost of his true self? Or what can he give that will buy that self back? For the Son of Man is to come in the glory of his Father with his angels, and then he will give each man the due reward for what he has done." (Mt 16:24-27).

The wrong Self is the root cause of all our troubles, and getting rid of it is liberation. As easy as that. Before we could get too confused or mystified, Tony quoted the Lord's words to St. Catherine of Siena: "I am he who is; you are she who is not." That is the truth we have to realize. We are not. We as we are not. I as I am not. I am so accustomed to see myself as myself that this may not be easy for a start. The first step will be to understand with the mind what this exactly means, and then the much more important and much more difficult step will be to accept, to assimilate, to realize that inward truth and to live accordingly thereafter. Let us proceed by parts.

Tony stood in the middle of the group that sat in a wide circle in the famous "Sadhana chairs," very comfortable reclining chairs which eased the stiffness of our bones during the long daily sessions, took a chair in his hand, showed it around, and said, "If I say 'this chair' and I say 'my chair,' is there any difference? Certainly not to the chair. Nothing has changed in the chair by my calling it 'mine.' Where nature is concerned, there is no 'mine.' If I'm annihilated, this chair remains the same. The 'my' adds nothing to the chair; it is a pure convention in our head. And the same goes for my community, my country, my family, my friends. Buddha said these wise words: 'These are my sons, my house, my land . . . : those are the words of a fool who does not understand that even he is not his.' If the 'my' adds nothing when added to anything else, it adds nothing either when used on oneself. 'My' self means nothing."

Tony left the chair, took a book in his hand, and returned to the center of the group. "Look at this book. What is it made of? I can put it neatly as a mathematical equation: Pages plus print plus cover plus pictures equals book. Clear? But suppose I say, Pages plus print plus cover plus pictures plus book equals book. Something wrong with that, isn't there? I have smuggled the word 'book' into the definition of 'book.' That will never do. Any logician will at once detect the fallacy and point out that I cannot define a book by a book. Vicious circle. Well, now watch. Here is Kurien [one of the men in the group]. What is he made of? Now, of course, different theories will say different things; some will say that he is made of earth, water, wind, and fire, others of molecules, atoms, electrons, or of mind, body, and soul, or, as we prefer to say, simply of body and soul. So there we have our equation: Body plus soul equals Kurien. But that is not what we say. We say, Body plus soul plus Kurien equals Kurien. We introduce the person of Kurien into Kurien's definition. We put an 'I,' a 'self' on top of his body and soul and different from them, that is, we put 'Kurien' into 'Kurien,' we make Kurien own and control

Kurien, and thereby get him into an identity trap out of which he may never quite extricate himself.

After saying that the example of the book was the clearest way he had so far found to explain this, Tony went on: "Remember what the Irishman asked his parish priest, 'When I die, my body will be in the grave, and my soul in heaven; but . . . where will "I" be?' We overstress that little "I" and we imagine it as someone who sits at the back of our skull, owns our mind and body, feels responsible for them, controls them, and so it becomes an 'I' controlling 'me,' which is an impossible bind. Think of the expression, 'I have to save my soul.' Who is this 'I' that has to save 'his' soul? Someone different from the soul, isn't it? Otherwise how could 'he' save 'it'? So we have put a self in charge of the soul. The self will save its soul. But who now, pray, will save the self? Obviously we have to put another self in charge of the first self. The second self will now look after the first self and eventually 'save' it. Now what about the second self? We have got ourselves into an infinite tangle. A room with a thousand mirrors. Illusion after illusion. Unless we get rid of the first self there is no way out of the labyrinth.

"Or look at it this way. The mind has invented the first 'I.' That has created a duality between the 'I' and the soul. We call that duality the opposition between my true self and my lower self, the old man and the new, the top dog and the underdog . . . in different terminologies, both in spirituality and in psychology. But once that duality has been established, someone has to be put in charge of it to judge and rule and control. Another 'I,' and yet another and another without end. A whole hierarchy of 'I's in our brain. Sheer madness. The watcher being watched by the watcher who is being watched by . . . nothing to end up with. No way out of the impasse except preventing it from happening at all, that is, denouncing the fallacy of the first 'I.'

"Have you ever heard a more insane term than the term 'self-control'? What does it mean? That the self controls the self? That the self controls something else? Or that something else controls the self? Just crazy. 'I blame myself.' Who blames whom? Am I split down the middle for a half of me to blame the other half? 'I have to take myself in hand.' Whose hand, if I may know? If it is your hand, it is your self's hand too, isn't it? You'll have quite a job catching your hand with your same hand. Or, as Alan Watts says, biting your teeth with your teeth, seeing your eye with your eye (no mirror), or touching the tip of your right index finger with the tip of your right index finger. A thankless task. And yet we are all engaged in it heart and soul. Self-improvement, self-denial, self-determination. But who improves whom, who denies whom, who rules whom? Eternal merry-go-round which makes impossible all real progress unless we break out of it."

All of Tony's histrionic talents, which were considerable, were needed to hold our attention while he spoke, acted, gesticulated, raised his voice, mimicked, and clowned addressing now one, now another in the perplexed group. The group listened with intent determination, though the intensity of the listening was not matched by the perspicuity of the understanding. I could see doubtful pencils poised over blank notebooks, the blank pages reflecting the blank minds which ostensibly were finding it difficult to think quickly along unfamiliar lines. Tony lowered his sights and became more descriptive.

"The 'I' is only a label attached to this body-soul complex. I am an organism called Tony. That's all there is to it. The trouble is that the label hides the reality, and, as we usually do, we take the label for what it signifies, the map for the territory, the name for the thing. We give the label an independent existence and we believe that the 'person' of Tony is something existing by itself independently of his body and soul and ruling both. Let us try to defuse the situation by referring to ourselves as 'organisms' with only our names attached to them. We'll have some fun." He then addressed himself to Joe Puli, Jesuit Provincial of Kerala, and told him, "Suppose I tell you now, pointing at you, 'I've heard that *this organism* is doing a pretty good job as Provincial.' How do you feel? You like it, of course, but you don't feel particularly elated by that statement of mine. Whereas if I tell you, 'I hear that *you* are doing a good job as Provincial,' you feel greater satisfaction, right? In the same way, if I tell you, 'I hear you're doing a poor job as Provincial,' you'll surely feel it, whereas if I say, 'I hear this organism is doing a poor job as Provincial,' you'll not be so badly affected. You see the point. The direct 'I' or 'you' is threatening because it takes itself very seriously as the ultimately responsible for all that 'your organism' does or fails to do. As soon as we drop the threatening label, the intensity of feeling, positive or negative, subsides. I've found I can tell a man with impunity, 'Your unconscious is a bastard,' to which he'll agree with a smile, while if I tell him, 'You are a bastard,' he may react violently and I may have to take shelter. The devaluation of the 'I,' even if it is only verbal, already brings about a great relaxation and easiness in dealing with any situation. St. Theresa was given the grace to see herself as though she were an outsider to herself, to feel disidentified from herself, and thus to achieve the supreme peace of not being affected by whatever happened to her, good or bad, since it felt as though it were happening to someone else."

I thought then of Swami Ramdas, the lovable Hindu mystic who always spoke of himself in the third person as the most natural thing, considering almost as happening to someone else whatever happened to him. With anybody else that would have seemed artificial and farfetched, but with him it sounded most natural and obvious. There was no sense of self in him, and so there was no first person in his language. St. Paul had said in the most sublime expression, "I live, no, not I; Christ lives in me." The highest religious experience in all ages and climates seems to be linked to this release from the narrow limit of the self into a higher consciousness, however this can or cannot be described.

I then voiced an objection which I thought was in the minds of many in the group: "I go along with seeing myself as 'this organism,' but then, Tony, if this organism called Carlos has a toothache 'I' feel something which I do not feel when that organism called Tony has the toothache." Tony made the point clear: "What I have said about disengaging yourself mentally from your own self refers to everything except physical pain. Take the example of an animal that has no psychological sense of being a 'person.' It feels animal pain and reacts to it, and in that we are exactly like it. Animal pain is felt in the organism, and the appropriate reaction sets in. That is as it should be. But not so with any other kind of pain or sensation. Suppose you are insulted. Here is where your organism must feel entirely indifferent, as though it had been Tony's organism that had been insulted. So long as you feel the insult, there is some 'I' left in you."

I got the point, but urged on in the same line: "What happens when I die, that is, when this organism dies?" Tony answered in a flash, "There is no I, Carlos. Nobody dies. There is no death." I sensed a hush in the hall. These were deep waters indeed.

Tony was in dead earnest. He meant every word he said, he spoke with zeal and conviction; it was evident that whatever he was saying was the result of long reflection and personal experience. I remembered that already in the Poona days of Sadhana I he had briefly mentioned the mystery of the self, and had once formulated the direct question, "After all, what is the 'I'?" This shows that the thought must have been with him since those early years, though he did not elaborate on it then; and it was now, after ten years of study and practice in his own persevering way, that the seed had given fruit, and the brief question had become the core of his teaching.

In *The Song of the Bird* there are also some indications of this line of thought. I quote one story which is called precisely "Dropping the 'I' ": "Disciple: 'I have come to offer you my service.' Master: "If you dropped the "I", service would automatically follow." (Commentary:) You could give all your goods to feed the poor and your body to be burnt and yet not have love at all. Keep your goods and abandon the 'I'. Don't burn the body: burn the ego. Love will automatically follow."

Those words, "burn the ego," summarize the practical aspect of Tony's teaching. His expressions are sometimes overenthusiastic and verge on the ontological level, as though in reality there was no "I," no person to bear the responsibility of choice and to carry on the identity of individual consciousness through life and into eternity. Language fails all mystics when they try to express their experiences, and Tony's efforts to achieve clarity where no clarity can be achieved may appear strange and confusing if isolated from the whole of his practice and personality. When, however, this teaching is focused on its psychological and spiritual aspect, it acquires its true importance and urgency as the basis and center of our spiritual life and ascetical effort to come out of "ourselves" and approach God.

All spiritual writers agree, and our experience confirms their verdict, that our selfishness is the root of all the evil we do and of all the suffering we endure. Only a truly selfless person can be really loving, pure, dedicated, open in service to all men, and devoted in worship to God. The Baptist's motto "he must increase and I must decrease" is the fundamental rule of life for all those who want to prepare the ways of the Lord and announce his presence. And every Jesuit treasures the essential words of his order's founder St. Ignatius at a turning point in his *Spiritual Exercises:* "Each one will profit in all spiritual things in the measure in which he goes out of his own self-love, self-will and self-interest."

In a way there was nothing particularly original in Tony's doctrine; but what gave an edge and thrust to his words was the strength of his own conviction and the genuineness of his personal experience. He did communicate to us something of the enthusiasm and eagerness he felt for what he clearly saw to be the highest pursuit of man on earth. And now came the unavoidable questioning of his keen listeners: How do we go about it in practice?

Here Tony suddenly grew cold, distant, almost detached from his eager audience, in an obvious technique which was telling us with the almost callous indifference of a Zen master: That's your lookout; I've shown you the way, and now it is for each one to walk the best he can; you know me enough and my Sadhana ways, and need not be told that nobody will do for you what you alone can do: to live your life. He spoke in negative terms, as all mystics do when they reach these heights, but the very negation is meaningful and helpful since, by closing easy doors, it forces us happily to try the difficult ones.

This is what Tony said when he came to explain how to put in practice the vital truth he had explained: "No effort, however strong and courageous, will lead us to the dropping of the self. In fact, all effort here is contraproducing, because it reinforces the self. Any discipline based on will-power will have the effect of strengthening the self, and thus will defeat its own purpose. The eternal paradox we have already met that without effort we can do nothing, and with effort we spoil everything. The only way out is to open our eyes and see. See, realize, let the scales fall from our eyes. Precisely because it is easy it is so difficult. This spirituality is not for all. Even among those who embrace it, one in a million reaches the final illumination. And, let us not fool ourselves, this illumination is all or nothing; it is not obtained by parts; you cannot be 'rather pregnant,' either you are or you are not. Though the reason that few attain it is simply that few desire it. Again we meet here the initial fact that 'nobody wants to be healed,' nobody in fact wants to be released from his own narrow self; it looks too frightening and strange to venture into that hidden realm. We all want to keep a hold on ourselves, and so we miss the promise of the final liberation. If we would release that hold on ourselves, the way would open for us. Even the ultimate end would certainly be attainable for all of us here under grace. And the fact of living somehow in this atmosphere, even without the supreme enlightenment, is already pacifying and refreshing beyond measure. Start walking that way and you'll experience it."

It is not only the great religious trends in the world that converge on that noble endeavor of the war on the egocentric self, but, surprisingly and reassuringly, modern psychology and psychotherapy have also discovered that the root of all human troubles is precisely that persistent and obstinate self, and that, therefore, the return to sanity requires the thoughtful downgrading of the overvalued self. A book that passed from hand to hand those days in Lonavla was the delightful little treatise *Simply Sane* by Gerald May, some of whose ideas have already appeared in Tony's words, and others I quote here directly:

Belief in "self" is far more than a simple mistake in logic or an expedience in language. It does real damage. Sensing a self which somehow possesses and manipulates body, mind and soul, these become objects. They become things and lose their wonder. Even that might be tolerable if we stopped there, but we don't. Sensing that the "self" is ultimately responsible for controlling the rest of the person, what happens when some part gets out of control? When a mistake is made? When one fails to get what one wants? Then we begin to feel that our "self" is somehow deficient because it didn't do a good job. Then comes a veritable avalanche of delusions. If the self isn't working right, it needs to be controlled and improved upon. A self, which can't be found, sets out to control that very same self. Incredible, but it goes even further. When one is successful, when one does what one wants, when things are "under control", who takes the credit? Who swells with pride and glory? That same elusive self. "I did a good job." Who did? "I am in control of myself." Who is? Credit leads to pride, and blame to responsibility, keeping the delusion alive. The highest values of our society have bowed to this insanity. Humankind is now at a point where the self cannot be given up. The self cannot be killed because it cannot be found. Accept it as part of the human condition. Even find love for it. With acceptance and love, relaxation is possible, and one can rest for a while. And with relaxation and rest, a trust can begin to build. A trust that whatever the self is, it will take care of itself. A trust that behavior can remain responsible if one eases one's grip on the elusive steering wheel. A trust that deep and clear living happens when one ceases trying to live. . . . It has not always been this way. Human beings have not always felt that their selves were objects. There was a time when people were not concerned about the self. It was a time of simply being. It was a time after life became aware of living, but before the human will became drunk with power. In those days human beings felt nothing special about being human. Newborn people entered the world with no more fanfare than accompanied the hatching of a bird's egg or the sprouting of a flower. And when someone died it was no different than a leaf falling from a tree. . . . There is nothing wrong with a concept of self. The problem begins when the idea of self becomes mistaken for reality. And true insanity sets in with the feeling that one should build, fix, improve upon or otherwise control that thing. If one could go about life sensing that one's self is simply the name given to a particular collection of body, mind and soul, there would

be no great craziness. But we bring in "something" which exists
behind body, mind and soul, controls them and is responsible for
them . . . and the trouble begins.

Remarkable parallel between modern psychology and traditional religion. They all seem to agree that the self is the
villain of the piece. "God expects but one thing of you, and
that is that you should come out of your Self in so far as you
are a created being, and let God be God in you" (Meister
Eckhart).

The self has come to stay. It will not be easy for most
mortals to get rid of it. But at least we can lighten the burden by taking it easy, bringing down its importance and
letting it ride lightly on things. If we cannot dethrone the
tyrant entirely, let us at least curtail his powers. This is the
old piece of advice, "Don't take yourself too seriously,"
invested now with a new dignity on the basis of mysticism
and psychology. Tony himself, in spite of his all-or-nothing
attitude in this matter, came to admit that partial gains were
also possible, and any progress in that direction would bring
an increase of peace and depth in life, so as to make it
worthwhile for us to use whatever means may suggest themselves to understand, accept, assimilate the doctrine of the
non-self. That would be and remain for all of us the chief
aim of our Sadhana.

This heartening concession, however, must not in any
way blur the constant insistence which Tony brought to
bear, with all his engaging ways and his persuasive powers,
on the importance and gravity of this single-minded endeavor. He quoted St. John of the Cross and said that this
and nothing else was his famous "nothing, nothing, nothing" leading to the "all, all, all." The ceasing of the self is
the rock bottom of the "nothing" that brings in faith the
fullness of the "all."

It was during one of those eloquent attacks on the egocentric self, when nothing seemed to be left to do or not to do in the dark night of the soul, while Tony was ruthlessly hammering on this central truth, closing every escape and invalidating every excuse, and urging us on to total generosity in spite of the difficulties of the task that seemed to leave us suspended without support between heaven and earth, that I heard what was perhaps the most beautiful and meaningful sentence I ever heard from Tony's lips. He said, "When people hear me speak in this way they tell me, 'Tony, listening to you one is left with nothing to hang on to . . .'; and I then complete their sentence, adding in the same tone: '. . . as the bird said when it began to fly.' Now you know."

Doodles

If any of my readers gets the impression that this is an easy book for me to write, he or she will be greatly mistaken. For one thing, there is my constant preoccupation to be faithful to Tony's thought as well as to my own interpretation of it, conscious as I am that this book will be mostly read by people who knew Tony, who have listened to him or have read his books and so have formed in their minds their own image of Tony, will expect to see it reflected in this book, and will be disappointed if they don't find it or, worse, find it distorted or substantially different from what they hold it to be. This book will have as many censors as readers, and that thought has sometimes stayed my hand and has made me rewrite more than one page.

And, for another thing, Tony was the most disorderly speaker it has been my privilege to listen to in all my life. If I have managed to order my chapters till now and keep different topics under different headings, that has been only as the result of a persistent and painstaking effort to ensure clarity of exposition and progress of thought. Tony did nothing of the kind. He spoke of each one of those topics in each one of the sessions, mixing them happily as occasion came, jumping from one to another without notice, changing direction at the slightest hint, always reacting to the here-and-now with utter disregard for any systematic order or any semblance of completeness of any kind. He appointed a man in the group (my charming friend Tony Matta) to take note whenever he said, "Remind me to take up this point with you later on," and to keep reminding him of the loose ends in subsequent sessions. The result was that the assurance that he was going to be reminded made him even more carefree in his ramblings; and no reminders, however efficient, could keep up with his new digressions and digressions within digressions. My own notes bear witness, line by line, to the spontaneous disorder of his creative thought.

Faced with that situation, I have made my procedure to select what I thought were the main topics he dealt with in those days, comb my notes for all references relative to each topic, and order them somehow under the corresponding heading. After I've done that in all the past chapters, I still find a number of stray thoughts left out like doodles on a printed page, and I want to collect some of them here without any particular order or connection. No attempt at completeness moves me to do that, but only the reluctance to leave out some things I enjoyed Tony saying.

"Are you upset because you have misplaced your keys? Cheap solution: Get up and find the keys. Real solution: Get in touch with your upset feelings, stay with them, accept them till they settle down and you achieve peace. Then by all means get up and locate the missing keys. You'll need them in any case."

"Take things in and apply them to yourselves. Don't simply take notes with the idea of telling these things to others and remain untouched yourselves. A parish priest was once preaching a thundering sermon to his parishoners: 'You all will die, and everyone in this parish will come face to face with the Eternal Judge and will have to give an account of all his life with all his sins in it, and suffer the punishment God will impose on him for them. Fear and tremble!' While the congregation shuddered in unison, a man in the benches started laughing out loud, in contrast to the universal consternation. The parish priest rebuked him from the pulpit: 'Are you out of your senses that you alone don't recognize the seriousness of the situation?' The man answered, 'But I don't belong to this parish!' Well, we all are in the same parish here."

"Sometimes a truth is best expressed by a lie. Once a man was dying and in his last moments expressed a desire to see his only son. The son was located, fetched, arrived when the dying man had lost his power to see and talk, but could still hear and sense. The son went straight to him, but on approaching him and seeing his face he realized that the dying man was not his father. There had been a mistake, and it was too late to correct it. What was he to do? He reacted quickly. He took the dying man's hand into his, leaned close to his ear, and told him lovingly, 'Daddy, I've come. I am your son. Here I am by your side.' A smile of bliss lighted up the dying man's face, and he died in peace. Was that a truth or a lie?" Tony then told an even more vivid story to make the same point, but that story is not printable.

A story with second intentions . . . very much in Tony's line. "A man was going daily to buy his newspaper from a newsstand whose owner was so surly that while selling him the newspaper, he insulted and abused him daily. A friend of the victim's noticed that and told him, 'Why do you insist on buying your newspaper from that news dealer who abuses you so badly each time? At the same distance from your house there is another newsstand whose owner is very kind and obliging and will be very happy to supply you with the newspaper every day without your having to endure the insults of that other madman." At that the victim of the insults answered, 'And why should that man, who according to you insults me, be the one who decides for me where I buy my newspaper?' Do you understand?"

I am not here to record all the stories our incomparable "storyteller" told us in Lonavla, but I'll mention my favorite one. Its seeming innocence hides courageous consequences in its application. Jesus also spoke in parables. "Let him who has ears to listen with, listen."

"A shepherd was grazing his sheep on the fields when a man approached him and started asking him questions about his sheep. 'Tell me,' he asked, 'how much do your sheep walk on an average day?' The shepherd replied, 'Do you mean the white ones or the black ones?'—'Well, the white ones.'—'About four kilometers.'—'And the black ones?'—'About four kilometers.' The man asked again, 'How much do they eat?'—'Do you mean the white ones or the black ones?'—'The white ones.'—'Some three kilos of grass.'—'And the black ones?'—'Three kilos too.' The man was beginning to get mystified, but went on with his questions. 'And how much wool do your sheep yield?' The shepherd was ready with his clarification. 'The white ones or the black ones?'—'Let's take the white ones first.'—'Five measures of wool a year.'—'And the black ones?'—'Five measures a year.' That was the end of the man's patience, and he exploded with understandable vehemence, 'Here I'm asking

you questions about your sheep, and every time you make
me ask separately about the white and the black, only to
give me afterwards exactly the same answer for both. Is
there any difference after all?'—'Of course there is, sir,' said
the shepherd with the knowing smile of a peasant's wisdom
on his lips. 'The white sheep are mine!'—'And the black
ones?' asked the man in his final curiosity. The shepherd
answered, 'Why, they also are mine,' the smile still on his
lips."

That story stood me in good stead the very same day I left
Lonavla. I stopped for the evening in Bombay on my way
back to Ahmedabad, and I gave a public address which had
been announced previously. In fact I had intended to prepare it in Lonavla, as I had anticipated I would have plenty
of free time those days. As it happened, I got so involved in
our Renewal that I did not prepare my Bombay talk. I faced
my audience only with a last-minute preparation, but such
was my personal joy and fullness fresh from Lonavla that my
inner happy excitement broke through to my audience right
from the start, and the two-hour talk became a memorable
experience. At the end there was a question-answer period,
with the questions sent in writing from the audience as it
was a large one. I read the first question, and a thrill of joy
shook my whole body and flowered on my lips. The question was, "Father, can you tell us the secret of the joy and
happiness we see bubbling in you today?" I kept the piece
of paper, and made a mental note to show it to Tony when
we met again. His death robbed me of the chance.

And now the use I made of his story. In the audience,
made up mostly of Jains (followers of Mahavir, contempo-
rary of Buddha and in some ways similar to him), there
were three Jain monks who started pressing on me their
own interpretation of the universe, which I know well and
which is one of the most systematically conceived and mi-

nutely classified of all philosophies. They repeated to me the list of their five "elements," four "types," seven "substances" with fourteen "sub-substances," and the endless litany of their scholastic categories. I was in a mischievous mood and, with a straight face to hide my intentions, asked their leader, "Maharaj-ji, how would it work if instead of putting seven substances we put . . . eight and a half!" He didn't see my joke, though everybody else did, and then to justify my lighthearted fun and appease the monks, I told them all the story of the white and the black sheep. All our mental distinctions turn out to be like the shepherd's distinctions. My audience enjoyed the story with me. The monks didn't.

"Never forget the advice our Goenkaji [who had directed a ten-day Buddhist Retreat for as at Igatpuri] was given by his own guru U Ba Kin: 'Your nose is your best friend.' Conscious breathing, attention to the breathing in and breathing out, being attuned to the rhythms of the body. That is the way to internal peace."

"Ignatius says, When eating, think of Jesus. Zen says, When eating, think of eating. Are these two approaches so different? Is not Jesus our food? Is not every food symbol of the Eucharist? Is not God present in all we eat? Is not every action of ours an act of faith? Do what you do, and eat when you eat. Jesus is with you."

"Do you know the story of the Italian wedding party? The new couple needed a place for the celebration after the ceremony, and, not being able to hire a hall and fearing possible rain for an open-air gathering, they requested the parish priest to allow them to have the celebration in the church itself after the religious ceremony. The parish priest finally agreed, not without some misgivings, and insisted on

the condition that there should be no drinking and no dancing in the church. The promise was willingly given . . .
and willingly broken. Who could conceive an Italian wedding without music and dance? The parish priest heard the
noise, went to stop it, but first informed his assistant of the
situation to enlist his help. The assistant made him reflect:
'Think of Cana of Galilee. Was that not a wedding party
with good wine and, no doubt, good dancing, in the very
presence of Jesus and Mary?'—'Yes', countered the reluctant parish priest, 'but the Blessed Sacrament was not there!'
Eyes to see Jesus."

"Be always loyal to the Church; she is our Mother. Not
only to the Church of the present but also to the Church of
the future."

"I am aware that some people hate me. One priest has
never forgiven me since I told him he was dealing with the
Holy Spirit as with a teddy bear. Others say I have a 'prima
donna' complex. I certainly like to be in the middle of
things, and occupy the center of the group in conversation.
On the other hand, I myself am surprised, and I can hardly
believe it though it is a fact, that I am simply not affected by
what other people say of me whether in praise or in denigra-
tion. It truly leaves me indifferent, and this was not so before."

"Religion is the finger pointed at the moon. Don't suck
the finger!"

Tony told the famous story of the Upanishads, but changing the tiger into a lion, a thing which I disliked and told
him so. It is true that there are a few lions in India in the Gir
forest in my state of Gujarat, but the universal wild animal
of India is the tiger, and to it refers the original story in all

its deep relevance to the doctrine of the true self. A tiger cub was lost in the forest, wandered into a herd of goats, and grew up with them eating grass like them, bleating like them, and thinking himself to be a goat. One day a tiger came upon the herd, saw the strange sight of a tiger like himself behaving like a goat, took it aside, and tried to convince it that it was a tiger, not a goat. No argument availed. The two tigers went to a pond where their faces were reflected and looked alike. And then the final proof. The real tiger killed a goat and made the goat-tiger taste blood. Then its whole true nature woke up within it, and with a mighty roar it went to join its kind. Tony justified to me his change of animal saying that he had first used the story in his talks in America, and there a lion, with its roar and its reputation as king of the forest, fitted in better for the story than a tiger. Small change in any case. The challenge of the story stands. The awakening of the true self (that is, the non-self).

I watched this little exchange between Tony and one of the group:—"That's a nice little tape recorder you have, Tony."—"Would it be of any use to you?"—"Yes, I was precisely looking for one like this."—"Then keep it. I can always get a new one when I need it. That is the advantage of traveling abroad often." There and then the tape recorder changed hands.

One of the women in the group, particularly good-looking, came to one of the sessions with her long hair let loose over her shoulders in the beautiful way typical of the women of Kerala in South India. I noticed it, and when the session was over I crossed the floor to where she was still sitting on her chair, bent level with her, and told her, looking straight into her eyes, "Thank you for letting your hair down. You look so very beautiful that way!" She smiled back her happy embarrassment, and I moved on. Tony had observed the little encounter from the other corner of the hall, and as I was coming out he asked me, "What did you tell her to make her smile so broadly?" I told Tony. He commented, "I bet you tomorrow she comes again with her hair down. I only hope she doesn't know the other meaning of the expression!"

The day you say, "Am I mad, or is everybody else mad?" that is the day your salvation has begun.

The Sadhana anthem to be sung on farewells to the tune of *"Ein Schneider hat'ne Maus"*: "We're sorry to see you go/ We're sorry to see you go/But what the hell are you doing here?/We're sorry to see you go."

I remarked to Tony how differently and unexpectedly he reacted to cases which to all appearances seemed quite similar. He answered me, "I depend on that for my success."

During one of my Renewals with him, Tony told me, "I read a good deal to know what is new and to revise the old, as also to cull new stories from all sources for my talks and my books. But for my own personal profit I read only three authors: Krishnamurti, Alan Watts, and Bertrand Russell." As regards Krishnamurti that represented a change in Tony. During my Sadhana I, I had asked him about his opinion of Krishnamurti and he had answered, "I don't think much of him." When I now reminded him of that, he said, "I must have read the wrong book or not given attention. Now I find him healthy, deep, and refreshing." I had had two long personal interviews with Krishnamurti, and Tony questioned me in detail about them and about my impression of him as a person. He was not impressed by his biography, but very much by his writings, or rather his talks. To such an extent that in Lonavla some days he came to the session with a book of Krishnamurti's and started reading out to us from it, commenting phrase by phrase on the text as the basis for his whole talk. That was certainly an unusual procedure with Tony, and shows the appreciation he had reached for Krishnamurti's thought. He also told us that if anybody now wanted to do a personal Retreat (eight days of silent meditation) under him, his method was to give the retreatant a book by Krishnamurti (preferably *Think on These Things,* or *This Matter of Culture* as it is called in its London edition, which, as it is made up of talks to students, is more understandable) and ask him to read a chapter a day and to come to comment on it with him. He acknowledged that it takes a good amount of concentration and reflection to get to his meaning sometimes, though it is worth trying. A quotation we both enjoyed: "Every effort is a distraction from the IS." Food for thought.

"Anytime you complain against anyone, you are saying you are better than him."

"I used to tell you, Give 'positive strokes' to people to make them feel good whenever they do something positive. Now I tell you, Don't do such thing, except for socially polite expressions of formal support. Positive strokes are only a subtle manipulation to make the other person dependent on your praise and docile to your expectations."

"When the weather in Lonavla is too hot, as it is happening these days, I feel guilty and apologetic about it, as though it were 'my' climate. See what extremes we can reach by mistakenly identifying ourselves with things that have nothing to do with us and over which we have no control. That is exactly what happens with the imaginary self."

"Serious doctors in the States have told me that placebos work as efficaciously as the actual medicine . . . right up to its side effects, which are unknown to the subject under experimentation. Isn't it frightening to realize the power of the mind over the body?"

"Welcome to the human race!" was Tony's spontaneous outburst when some troubled man or woman hesitatingly mentioned some personal weakness which we all knew was only too common.

The Sadhana Way of Life

Toward the end of my nine-month Sadhana in Poona, I made a suggestion in the group which was badly received by all. I said, "We've been here for almost a year, living together through an intimate spiritual experience which has changed our lives, and in the course of that experience we have often expressed new principles, ideas, approaches, and have used words and sentences which now mean much to us, and which sum up between themselves the spirit we have learned and we want now to carry into our lives and to practice in our daily behavior. It could be a good idea to collect now all those key phrases, each one making his or her own list, collating them and coming out with a fair sampling that would reflect our present thinking, remind us of our convictions, and help us to live up to them. Do you like the plan?"

No, they didn't. They thought an experience can never be put down on paper, the letter kills while the spirit gives life, a set of formulas would look like an esoteric charter, open to misunderstanding and abuse by anyone into whose hands it would fall. Even Tony was against the idea, but never quite closed to any kind of initiative, he said finally, "Let's give it a try." We did. Each one wrote there and then a list of such phrases and read it out. They sounded good. A consensus of pointed sentences emerged, and we completed each other's lists. They all felt happy, and Tony said, "After all it was a good idea. Let us call it. 'The Sadhana Way of Life.'" There was no official statement and no list was printed; but I have my list with me, and I want to quote its main items with brief comments, as much of it remains valid and was taken for granted by Tony even in subsequent elaborations of his thought. Each one of these sayings had, at one time or another, made very much sense to him.

"Lose your mind and come to your senses." That was the starting point of all his considerations. We have given too much importance to our mind in our lives, and too little to our senses. Thought is supposed to be the highest activity of the human being, while he shares his senses with the lower animals, and so the senses are neglected, mistrusted, despised. Thus we lose the "animal wisdom" which is nature's own wisdom, basis and guide of all subsequent wisdom in man. We have become truly "senseless" in the worst sense of the word, we are blind and deaf, have lost our capacity to see and to hear and to sense and to wonder, and have drifted into a dull routine we call existence, and then complain life is not worth living. It is time we come back to our senses and rediscover the multicolored beauty of life.

"The glory of God is man fully alive." This is a free quotation from St. Ireneus, much in favor with all modern renewal movements, which expresses beautifully a very consoling truth of faith. God has created me for his own glory, and, therefore, my only way of giving him glory is to ensure that this creation of his which is me should be the best possible within unavoidable limitations, that is, that I may become fully alive, fully myself. Psychologists tell us we all live far far below our possibilities, and use only a minimal percentage of our energies. Our aim is to raise our level of existing to higher perspectives in nature and in grace; to become fully alive in order to give full glory to God.

"Sharpen your wants, express them, and leave the other person free." Tony asserted this was the way he himself had grown through many years. To know what I want, that is, to allow myself to realize what it is that I really want, to feel it keenly, then to manifest it simply to the person from whom I want it, leaving him at the same time entirely free to grant my wish or refuse it. This is an exercise in self-knowledge, freedom, humility, courage, and sincerity. The wonder is, Tony insisted, that most of the times we ask a concrete thing from a concrete person, we get it. And if we don't get it, we have lost nothing. And in any case we grow in clarity and strength. He also applied the principle to spiritual discernment in a parallel saying: "To find out what God wants of you, first find out what you want of him."

"Be in touch with your feelings." That was Sadhana's first commandment. Uncover them, own them, face them, stay with them. Don't discriminate between "good" and "bad" feelings to accept some and reject others. Feelings in themselves are neither good nor bad. They are feelings, and the best way to drain them to harmlessness or to channel them to usefulness is to allow them to come up without censoring or suppressing them. I am angry, I am fearful, I am excited. I watch my anger or fear or excitement, my compassion or affection or pain, and then I decide in freedom what course of action I want to take. For all that it is essential that I keep in touch with my own feelings, and it is this constant touch that makes me come alive as a human being. Thought alone tends to regiment my life. Feelings bring variety, depth, warmth, and liveliness. To operate at "gut level" was the accepted way among us. For the "brain level" a more colorful language was used.

"Acceptance—empathy—congruence." The terms come from Carl Rogers and express the practical positive attitude to interpersonal relationships of any kind. *Acceptance* is the "unconditional positive regard" which never judges, possesses, or manipulates in any way the other person. *Empathy* is the ability to see and feel things as from the inside of the other person, and to communicate that understanding. *Congruence* is the permanent awareness of one's own feelings toward the other person, and the readiness to manifest them if that would seem advisable. Three words that embody a whole program of personal training and social responsibility.

"Awareness—spontaneity—intimacy." Three more words, this time from Eric Berne's own summary of optimal human behavior. The difficult art of *awareness* that makes the whole of me present and available to the whole of me, together with the whole universe of circumstances that surround me instant by instant far and near, for me to react to with paradoxically natural and cultivated *spontaneity* that brings freshness and sharpness to life, in pursuit of the adventure of *intimacy* where life itself flowers in all its unique splendor. These key words acquire a great meaning and a kind of affective glow when used daily and heard daily from people engaged in the same quest with the same enthusiasm.

"Break your own image." We are all slaves to the image we have created of ourselves and have projected on the world outside for people to have of us. If it is a "bad" image, as of a lazy, irresponsible, unreliable person, people will continue to look on us as lazy, irresponsible, and unreliable, and we ourselves will continue to be what people expect us to be, and to behave the way people expect us to behave. And if it is a "good" image, as of a serious, punctual, hardworking person, we'll continue to be serious, punctual, and hardworking, if not out of virtue at least out of the need to conform to the universal expectation we have created. In any case the image inhibits spontaneity, hinders creativity, and stifles life. It may be good, for a change, to be unpredictable.

"That is your problem." This has been largely misinterpreted as a callous, insensitive, selfish disregard of everybody else in a totally unchristian way. That is sheer calumny. With us the saying summed up the healthy recognition of the fact that whatever I do and will do for the others, they remain ultimately responsible for their actions, and I must not make myself miserable because someone I care for chooses to make himself or herself miserable. "I have long ago resigned from the job of general manager of the universe," Tony liked to say.

"The Sabbath was made for man, not man for the Sabbath." Respect all laws, but remember the Catholic teaching that the ultimate judge of the concrete action is the personal conscience at the moment of acting. Form your conscience and follow it.

"The trees become trees again." This is the ending of a famous saying by Ch'ing Yuan which I heard Tony repeat innumerable times through all the stages of his spiritual ministry. It says in full, "Before man's conversion takes place, the mountains are mountains for him, and the trees are trees. During the period of conversion, mountains for him are no longer mountains, and trees are no longer trees. After his conversion, mountains become mountains again, and trees become trees again." Once the soul and the body and the senses and the whole of man is purified, the whole of creation is given back to him, for him to enjoy in peace and happiness as permanent heritage of the children of God.

"Trying is lying." This is Fritz Perls. To say "I'll try" means that you don't seriously intend doing it. Say, "I'll do it" or "I won't." That is straight talk.

"Free the 'playful child' in you." We all carry within us a charming, loving, mischievous, joyful child which later constraints have confined to silence and oblivion. To release it and allow it free play is a secret of happiness.

"I should," "I must," "I have to" are expressions to be replaced by "I want," "I like," "I choose"—that is, when we really want and like and choose to behave that way.

"Your yes has no value unless you are free to say no."

"To make mistakes is our birthright."

"Don't push the river." That is again Fritz Perls, with Barry Stevens borrowing the phrase for the title of her autobiography. Don't push the river . . . it flows by itself. And so does life. Don't push. Barry Stevens again: "Happiness is letting the happenings happen."

"Get rid of your 'Please me' driver. "Drivers" are inborn or acquired tendencies to behave compulsorily in a particular way, and the tendency to please everybody can be strong in some people and defeats its own purpose in all. Whoever wants to please everybody ends up by displeasing everybody . . . including himself.

"Make good contact: with yourself, with people, with the world, with God."

"Have no expectations; and if you ever expect something from somebody, tell him."

"Sensitivity is the flower of charity."

"Accept chaos for order, insecurity for security, and uncertainty for certainty." The age of certainty is over. Welcome to the age of uncertainty.

"Holiness is wholeness." Recover all the parts of your personality you have lost along the years.

"Nobody ever grew without taking risks."

"My vineyard is mine to give" (Song of Songs).

"Believe the Good News." And the Good News is: "I have come that you may have life . . . to the full!"

"And God said, 'It's all very good indeed.' "

The Therapist

Tony was a healer. He had the compassion to sense the presence of pain in the soul of man, the unfailing eye to diagnose in a flash the root of evil, and the charismatic competence to bring relief through professional means to the troubled person. He was a great listener, a keen observer, a gifted surgeon of souls. I have watched him numberless times at work as a therapist, and want to give here a glimpse of that aspect of his which indeed shone through his whole personality, and where his whole personality was in turn reflected.

He appreciated all methods, particularly Carl Rogers's "non-directive counseling," but found it too slow for his own active temper. He expressed his criticism of the method in the story of the client and the non-directive therapist. The client: "I am depressed." The therapist: "So, you are depressed."—"I actually feel like committing suicide."—"I hear you say you would like to commit suicide."—

"Yes, in fact I am thinking of throwing myself out of that window just now."—"If I understand you well, you are just now contemplating throwing yourself out of that window." The client goes to the window and throws himself out of it. "Plop!" The therapist looks out of the window and repeats, "Plop!" The interview is over.

In practice Tony used Gestalt therapy, though, of course, his own brand of Gestalt. Straight to the point. What is your problem? Give me your feeling. Positive? Negative? Confused? Stay with the confusion. Let me guess. You are angry at yourself for having been too slow in reacting while all the others were quick, and you have cut a poor figure. Yes? Repeat that yourself. Louder. Does it fit? Fine. Now let's start the dialogue. Place your "slow" self in front of you, imagining he is seated on that empty chair that faces you, and letting now your "angry" self talk to him from where you are seated. That's the way. Your "angry" self is scolding your "slow" self. Tell him all that comes to your mind and in the strongest tone you can. Don't spare him. Good. Satisfied? Now let your "slow" self answer; he must also have his chance; that is, go and sit now on the chair where the "slow" self is seated and answer from there in his name. He also has full right to be heard, because he also is you. That is the dialogue. Understood? Listen very carefully to what you are telling yourself, as your "slow" self answers your "angry" self. Now come back to the first chair, be your "angry" self again, and keep up your complaints. Change chairs and keep up your answers. Enough of it? Nothing more to reproach or to answer? Good. How do you feel now? You have realized, no doubt, that your "slow" self had a point, and has full right to be slow when it wants to be slow, doesn't it? I see you are more at peace now. Stay with the good feeling. Another problem anyone?

You feel uneasy with So-and-so in the group. Don't tell me, tell him. Don't talk about people but *to* people. Tell him directly: "What I dislike in you is . . ." Give the whole list. Watch your own feelings while you say that. Fear? Apprehension? Relief? Do you feel reluctance to say what you are saying? Do you realize that as you verbalize some of your grievances they sound hollow even to yourself? Now get the other man's feelings. Don't argue, don't explain, don't defend yourselves and don't attack. Just express feelings. If you say, "You are wrong," you have started an argument, while if you say, "I feel pained when I hear you say that," you have opened a door. Keep the exchange at feeling level.

If a person in the group wanted to work out some similar tension situation with someone else who was not in the group, even some character in his or her past life, absent or even dead by then, there was always the possibility of dealing with the problem through fantasy work. Tony asserted that fantasy was one of the most powerful tools of therapy, and used it with impressive effectiveness. A woman was grieving because in her youth she had been rather insubordinate and had given a hard time to her mother, she had then left her to join the religious life though she was needed at home, later came to India as a missionary Sister, and when her mother died in her home country she had not been present at her death. Tony handled her grief with delicate care. Imagine your mother in front of you, alive as when you knew her, sitting on that chair and looking at you. Tell her now how much you feel the way you let her down, ignored her feelings, and missed her last blessing in her deathbed. Take your time about it. And now you yourself take your mother's part and answer what she would answer to you after all you have told her. (It was touching to see how the same woman who had blamed herself for being harsh and neglectful of her mother, when speaking now on behalf of her mother would say movingly, "Don't worry, my daughter; I know all that in my heart and I knew it then.

You were following your own ideals in the service of the Lord, and I had made my sacrifice for him . . . and for you. All I want is for you to be happy. Don't grieve over me anymore.") Tears would follow freely, and an old wound would close. Those were truly healing moments, not only for the woman who had come forward with her hidden anguish but for each one of us in the group. That was the way Sadhana worked, through direct therapy on ourselves, through empathic witnessing of therapy on others, and then, and very much so, through the intervening pauses and breaks and holidays during which the emotional inputs sank deep and worked themselves into our subconscious to create a new awareness and a new sensitivity to life. Nine months is a long time, and much silent growth was bound to take place in that privileged setting.

Tony granted great importance to fantasy work with us as a healing process, and began developing a number of fantasy exercises which he gave us regularly in the group, followed always by feedback on what we had felt through them, interchange of experiences, and working on problems which may have arisen out of the experiment. These exercises, without the live follow-up, of course, can now be found in the "Fantasy" part of Tony's first book, *Sadhana: A Way to God.* Here is a sample:

A sculptor has been engaged to make a statue of you. The statue is ready and you go to his studio to have a look at it before it appears in public. He gives you the key to the room where your statue is so that you can see it for yourself and take all the time you want to examine it alone.

You open the door. The room is dark. There, in the middle of the room is your statue, covered with a cloth . . . You walk up to the statue and take the cloth off . . .

Then you step back and look at your statue. What is your first impression? . . . Are you pleased or dissatisfied? . . . Notice all the details in your statue . . . How big it is . . . what material it is made of . . . Walk around it . . . see it from different angles . . . Look at it from far, then come closer and look at the details . . . Touch the statue . . . notice whether it is rough or smooth . . . cold or warm to the touch. What parts of the statue do you like? . . . What parts of the statue do you dislike? . . .

Say something to your statue . . . What does the statue reply? . . . What do you say in return? . . . Keep on speaking as long as you or the statue have something to say . . .

Now become the statue . . . What does it feel like to be your statue? . . . What kind of existence do you have as the statue? . . .

I want you to imagine now that, while you are your statue, Jesus walks into the room . . . How does he look at you? . . . What do you feel while he looks at you? . . . What does he say to you? . . . What do you reply? . . . Continue the dialogue as long as either Jesus or you have something to say . . .

After a while Jesus goes away . . . Now return to yourself and look at the statue again . . . Is there any change in the statue? . . . Is there any change in you or in your feelings? . . .

Now say good-bye to your statue . . . Take a minute or so to do this and then open your eyes. *

However much he appreciated and used fantasy work, Tony's greatest interest at the time was work with dreams. He granted dreams the greatest importance as an instrument for far-reaching therapy. He did not apply to dreams Freudian psychoanalysis but the Gestalt method of integration: to live the dream again and discover oneself in its meaning. A dream is a message from myself to myself, that is, a message that the sleeping self sends to the waking self with the intention to help it know itself better, discover itself, recover its lost aspects, and integrate the whole in a complete personality. Through my life I have been losing

* *Sadhana,* Image Books/Doubleday, 1985, pp. 87–88.

parts of my personality due to the conditionings imposed on me by others and by myself, the restrictions, prohibitions, pressures, fears. Fragments of my being have been scattered on the paths of my life, genuine and valid aspects of my personality which I myself have rejected and forgotten, but which are filed away in the shelves of my subconscious, and come back to life in the realm of dreams to remind me of their existence and ask for admission into my life again. Those parts of me which I have rejected, appear now in the dream projected into other objects and persons who are none other than myself, though I fail at first sight to recognize myself in them. Each image in my dream is some alienated part of me which I have to reown, to recognize and to admit in order to be myself again in all the fullness I can. The censorship of my mind during the day suppresses emotions, reactions, thoughts, instincts which are thus condemned not to see the light of day; but they take vengeance in the dark, and all that has been suppressed during the day comes up during the night in the distorted shapes of the realm of shadows. That is the dream. It is the "I" that I do not allow to be born. When I listen to my dream, I listen to myself. I learn to look and to see, I relive my dream fully awake now, I identify with those shadows, take their place, and speak through their mouths in the first person, recognizing myself in those canvases torn from my portrait, and reconciling the angel and the beast in me.

Tony began by telling us, "The therapist gets what the therapist asks for. I know that if I want dreams, you are going to come up with all sort of dreams daily. Bring them to me." We did. Since we all dream most of the time through our sleep, but forget the dreams that occur far from the waking periods, some of the eager initiates (not I!) took the trouble of setting the alarm clock to sound several times during the night, and kept paper and pencil under the pillow to jot down the dreams fresh from the night factory.

Thus the dreams reached the group, and then the procedure
was standard. Tell the dream. "I dreamt I was going alone
through a street, and there was an old house on it with its
door open, and a large hand came from behind and pushed
me to enter, and inside there was a staircase and the more I
climbed the more I went down, and I looked up and the
house had no roof, and on top of it was a big face that
looked down at me and laughed loudly when it saw me, and
I woke up." Now tell the dream again in the present tense
as though it was happening now. "I am walking alone along
a street and I see an old house. . . ." Now you are the
street; speak in its name. "I am the street. I am long and
deserted. I don't like people to walk on me. When anybody
walks on me, his steps make noise and I am hurt." Now you
are the house. "I am an old house of classic design. Knowl-
edgeable people know that my façade shows a noble style.
My foundations are strong. I know the histories of all the
people who have lived within my walls; yes, I understand
the lives of men better than many of them do." Now you
are the open door, the hand that pushes you, the staircase,
the large face that laughs, and . . . before that, as this is
important, you are also the roof that is missing from the
house: Speak in its name. This spontaneous and random
speaking from the mouth of the persons and objects in the
dream begins to uncover hidden corners of the past and to
return forgotten experiences to living memory. Then come
the questions to help the person himself to draw the conclusions he alone can draw. There is no question of "interpret-
ing" the dream but of "integrating" it into real life and into
the present moment to enrich and reestablish the whole person. What does all this tell you? What have you learned
about yourself? Have you got some light about some forgotten aspect of your life? What were you afraid of? An
important question (if the waking up had been natural,
without the alarm): What is for you the meaning of having

woken up at that particular moment and at that particular scene? And the fundamental question: What were you avoiding? This last question opened the door for startling discoveries in the mutilated personality, and led to growth and integration. We had ample opportunity to verify in ourselves and in our companions Freud's dictum that "dreams are the royal road to the unconscious." Tony enjoyed working with dreams, but the procedure was rather repetitious, and after some time the novelty wore off and he brought new resources to the always unpredictable content of the sessions.

The resource that never failed to liven up the group on any day and in any circumstance was the proposal of any of the numberless exercises he devised for us. "Stand up, all of you, men and women. Now each one of you silently place your right hand on the right shoulder of the person in the group you clearly like most. Start!" Can the reader imagine the flutter of feelings this order produced inside our chests? Move silently around. Whom do I choose? Do I know? Do I dare? Man or woman? Shall I play it safe? Safety doesn't pay around here. Take your risk and go straight. My hand has found its shoulder. Any other hands on that shoulder? And, with greater trepidation, how many hands on *my* shoulder? None? Oh, yes, I feel a touch. Thank God. Now let me take a look at the cluster of men and women standing silently, intensely, in a telling pattern of crisscross relationships. The trial is over. No, it's just beginning. "Now sit down all of you. Take a moment to gather your feelings. And now let's see. How did each one of you feel during the game? Apprehension? Shyness? Anger against me for making you do that? Jealousy? Insecurity? Resentment against someone? Or just enjoyment of it all in good fun? Come, who wants to speak first?" By then half a dozen hands were in the air, and the ensuing exchanges could take up the rest of the day.

Anything worse? Yes. The same exercise, but, instead of choosing the person we liked most . . . choosing now the person we liked least in the group! The whirlwind of feelings can be imagined. They supplied raw matter not for one but for several sessions after the game. And I can report a still harder one. Tony's directives were that day as follows: "Stand up, all of you, and without saying a word arrange yourselves in a straight line with its head near the window there, and its tail near the door. You yourselves choose the place in which you want to stand within the line according to this criterion: Where do I, as a person, stand in the group? If you honestly think you rate at the top, go and stand at the head of the line; and if you think you belong lower down, go and stand near the end. Allow for people to move freely as they wish, and don't say a word. Watch your feelings all the time." It took some time for the line to get stabilized, as people shifted positions till a sort of consensus was arrived at. Then Tony went on: "Now take a good look at the line, and if you see a man or woman who occupies in the line a position which you think is too high, bring him or her down to the position you think he or she should rightly occupy; or again bring up in the line those who in your opinion are too far down in it. In other words, put at the head of the line the man or woman in the group who, in your opinion, rates highest as a person, and so all the way down the line. Allow each one to work freely with the rest until stability is reached." No mean task! One could feel the unspoken tension build up in the room while the line changed and changed uneasily as different hands worked at it. Whom do I bring up? Whom do I move lower down? What will she think of me? How shall I explain that to her later? And . . . who dares to bring me down? Oh, that blackguard! And I thought he had a good opinion of me! We'll have to settle that later on. And for heaven's sake let's see when this ordeal gets over. At last. The human file is ready. Tony had not said a word while we moved around, but had not taken for a moment his keen eyes off the group to note down carefully in his mind all that each one of us was feeling during the experience. When we all finally stood still, he spoke: "Sit down and keep quiet for a while. Then we'll assess the damage. I know that some of you must be hurt to a greater or lesser degree, and I myself would not have put you through this experiment if I didn't have now nine months to heal the wounds it may have opened. Now give me your feelings, and let us work at them. Fire!"

Not all the exercises were as momentous as these, but all were directed, in one way or another, in serious earnest or in easy fun, to bring out our feelings, to break through our defenses, to expose the raw material of our personality hidden under so many layers of discipline, control, official masks, and stereotyped behavior. So far we had been taught to be the sort of persons we were supposed to be; now, without breaking with the past, but rather building on it and transcending it, we were learning to be the sort of persons we wanted to be. No wonder the process felt at times as exhilarating as a new birth . . . labor pains and all.

The point to emphasize is that these exercises, dreams or fantasies, had but little value in themselves. They acquired their importance only as instruments in Tony's hands. The valuable experience was not the exercise in itself, or the dream or fantasy, but the intense work that followed it in the intimacy of the group, with all the earnestness of the person who sought growth and healing, under the skill, the care, the charisma of Tony at his best. The experience was never to be forgotten.

Tony's uncanny power to guess people's feelings, to express unspoken thoughts, to figure out what was going on within a person before he or she said a word, manifested itself time and again in his daily person-to-person work in the group, and those incidents created and reinforced the

"Tony legend" about his mysterious powers to read people's minds. He himself contributed to the legend. He told us one day in the group, "I have recently discovered a new power in me. If I am surrounded by a number of people I have only to look at their faces to know exactly how each of them is feeling. I couldn't do that before, but now I know I can. The other day I tried it out with a number of young people around me, and I was right in each case." He certainly had unusual insights into people's minds, motives, and behavior, and in fact I kept going to him through the years to benefit from those insights. I enjoyed seeing myself reflected in his candid reaction, and was encouraged by his trust in me. Still, I personally do not believe he had any preternatural powers in the matter. I have reason to interpret some of his inexplicable guesses as the unconsciously obedient responses of people who, awed by his overpowering personality and his reputation as a mind reader, and unwilling to let Tony down before the group, said yes convincingly when Tony told them what they were thinking, even if in fact they were thinking something quite different. (It happened to me, so I should know!)

In this connection I have a good story to tell. The translator of Tony's works into Spanish, Jesús García-Abril, told me the surprising experience he had had with Tony. He had already translated several of his works and had corresponded with him over the matter, but they had never met. He took the opportunity of one of Tony's trips to Spain, and went to meet him in the city where he was going to conduct one of his courses. "There were dozens of people there," he went on, "as it was the opening day. Tony had never seen me in his life, not even a photo of mine; I, of course, recognized him and approached him to introduce myself to him. Imagine my surprise when, as I drew near, he looked at me and said first, 'You are García-Abril.' I was dumbfounded. To this day I cannot understand how he did it. The more I think of it the more inexplicable it looks to me. Have you any explanation for that?"

I hadn't at the moment, but a few months later I met Tony in Lonavla and told him the story. "You are getting quite a reputation as a wonder-worker," I teased him. He laughed wholeheartedly and said, "I remember the incident perfectly well. Now I'm going to tell you my version of the story. Yes, there were many people that day in that place, but I knew that two were coming from Santander, and one of them was García-Abril. They came to me when I was alone, and I knew those were the two people from Santander. One of them had to be García-Abril. It was then a fifty-fifty guess. I also knew from my correspondence with him that García-Abril was rather the artistic type, and of the two he clearly looked more like an artist. So I made my guess, and it turned out right. So much for my miraculous powers."

On the other hand, in all fairness, I have also to report another personal story which this time shook me, if only gently. We were one day in Sadhana telling jokes. This time, for a change, theological jokes. I am not much of a lad for telling jokes, but thought of one I had read somewhere and told it. A drawing depicts Moses taking down the decalogue from Yahweh, tablets and chisel in hand, and, when Yahweh has finished with the Ten Commandments, Moses looks up eagerly and says, "Lord, there is still room for one more!" Subtle Biblical humor. When the next round came I ventured to tell a joke I had invented myself and never told to anyone. All in the group knew the technical term that the Holy Spirit "proceeds" from the Father and the Son, and so they got the point at once and laughed approvingly. The story was that the Father and the Son were in disagreement over some matter or other, were getting excited over it, and decided to call in the Holy Spirit to act as counselor. The Holy Spirit listened to their heated arguments and then declared, "If you begin to quarrel in this way, how can I proceed?" Before the next man could tell his joke Tony looked at me and said, "Carlos, you have thought up that joke yourself, haven't you?" I said sheepishly, "Yes." True, the joke was bad enough, but how the hell did he know?

In any case Tony didn't need any legends. He was great enough without them.

The Spiritual Director

I'm working backwards. I began by describing the Lonavla experience (Sadhana II: Tony the guru), then outlined its background (Sadhana I: Tony the therapist), and now I want to complete the picture with the earlier and first stage of Tony's public work and personality: Tony the spiritual director. I was with him also in that period and got the full impact of the spiritual renovation he set in motion. The time is more distant, and the memories sketchy, but the veritable upheaval it caused in me is as much part of me as the latest Lonavla "bombshells," and I can write about it with conviction if not with detail. Here is a glimpse.

Tony's spiritual offensive (no other term would do justice to the concerted campaign Tony launched from his Vinayalaya headquarters) was a three-pronged attack on the comfortable routine to which most of us had settled in a surely active but spiritually unsatisfactory religious life. (He used to say at the time that provided a Jesuit was declared to be a hard worker, all defects and shortcomings could be forgiven him. Now it would seem that even the hard work has gone!) His three fronts were stark poverty, intense prayer, and direct experience of God.

His poverty drive struck the eye first. He abandoned the rather spacious room he occupied as rector of Vinayalaya and went to live in a cramped den under the staircase in obvious but happy discomfort. This was the external sign that ushered in the revolution. The "juniors" under him (young Jesuits under training after their "novitiate" and before their "philosophy") caught up readily with his enthusiasm and vied with one another in giving up more things and living more simply. Their ascetical exploits soon drew the attention of all Jesuits around, and praise and criticism began.

Poverty is necessary to imitate Jesus, to cultivate detachment, to renounce worldly power and so invite divine power in our apostolate ("when I am weak then I am strong"), to identify with the poor, to fight consumerism and achieve true availability as servants of the people. Ignatius had legislated that his followers should "eat, dress and be housed poorly," which meant plainly that they had to know hunger, wear worn-out clothes, and lack a proper bed. To explain the principle behind poverty Tony quoted his mentor Father Calveras in what (Tony claimed) was his only-ever attempt at humor. Calveras has said, "Aristotle established the principle that *'natura abhorret vacuum,'* that is, nature cannot leave holes, and when it sees a vacuum formed somewhere it rushes to fill it in. Well, God, of course, must have read Aristotle (that was the joke), and so when he sees a soul that has emptied itself of all possessions, attachments, and dependences, he rushes to fill that soul with his presence and his power." That was the principle, and Tony acted on it with all his irrepressible and contagious enthusiasm. The drive for total poverty was on.

Tony directed himself an eight-day Retreat for his own
community at Vinayalaya, and its impressive success made
him conceive the idea of announcing a thirty-day Retreat in
Khandala for any volunteers. This was unusual, as the thirty-
day Retreat is officially practiced by Jesuits only twice, once
at the beginning and once at the end of their formation.
Tony got together a small motley group, and the Long-Retreat movement was launched. I was there.

I will give an idea of Tony's uncompromising plea for
poverty by relating an incident that took place the day the
Retreat was over. We were all vociferously commenting on
the vicissitudes of those thirty days after the long self-im-
posed silence, when a jolly priest among us (who soon after
that left our company and married) took Tony up with
comic and indignant vehemence: "Look here, Tony. Everything else I can forgive you; but not what you said that day.
Remember? Day after day you were hammering on poverty, experiencing want, giving up everything, hard life, no
comforts, penance and fasting. For one week I lived on
bread and water following your recommendation, as many
others did too so that the cook complained that the food was
going to waste, and those who intended fasting each day
should give notice beforehand to the kitchen to calculate
the amount to be prepared that day. Fine. All that can be
tolerated. But not what you said after that. Remember? After all the pressure and the rigor you finally said one day,
'Well, of course, we all need a break also from time to time,
we need to relax, we need a holiday even from our
penances and mortifications, if only to come back to them
with greater zest again. Yes, we'll all do well to allow ourselves certain liberties occasionally, to have a good time, to
go wild for a while, yes, why not?, to do things we've never
done and really to enjoy ourselves. So, surely, if you feel
tired and want to give yourselves a break in life, go ahead,
feel free and . . .' While you were talking like that, Tony,

my mouth was watering and I was waiting in expectation what it was you were going to propose us to do in our wild moments, my imagination was running riot and I was thinking of, well, any mad thing, when you came to the climax and said, 'Yes, by all means, when you really want a break in life and feel the need for it, be generous with yourselves, and go and give yourselves . . . a good cup of tea!' *Tony!* Was that all you could think of by way of a break in life, a substantial relaxation, a wild adventure? A cup of tea! My foot! Now I know what I'm in for. One thing you can be sure of: You made your point quite clear to us. I will remember it whenever I drink a cup of tea!" That was the Tony of the cup of tea; as genuine as the Tony of the "celebrations of life" in later Sadhana.

The second point was prayer. "When I prescribe five hours of prayer daily," said Tony, "I mean it as a minimum, and, of course, without including the Eucharist, the breviary, the rosary, spiritual reading, and the examinations of conscience. And I don't mean this for the days of the Retreat, but for every day in the year. If we want to be men of prayer, we have to give time to prayer." We all did generously. Tony proved with scholarly exegesis that "consolation" (the Ignatian technical term for having a good time in prayer) should be the normal state of the soul in prayer, and so we were led not only to pray but to enjoy prayer.

This was clear and traditional teaching among Catholic spiritual masters, but had been largely forgotten, and we were exhorted to "pray in dryness," to "leave to children the milk of 'consolation,' and take the solid food of adults, which is 'desolation' in prayer" (this is a wrong and abusive interpretation of text of St. Paul's), or even, with Pascal, to "seek the God of consolations, not the consolations of God." False and dangerous doctrine. Tony made use here of his long and deep formation in Spain and Rome, and was able to quote with knowledge and authority from the great

Spanish classics to the modern exegetes of the Ignatian Exercises to whom he was much indebted.

One of them was, as I have mentioned, Calveras, and here is his doctrine on the point. To persevere in the spiritual life we need prayer, and to persevere in prayer we need to make prayer easy and joyful for us, and that is "consolation." This is the aim of the whole of the "fourth week" in the Spiritual Exercises, that is, "to establish the soul in a state of consolation" through the "office of consoler" assumed by Jesus in his resurrection, who now encourages his faithful "just as a friend consoles and encourages his friends." Another modern classic is Casanovas, who said on this point, "The spiritual authors who speak of consolations as though they were something accidental, as sweets and frills for children, do not know what they are talking about; they are not sweets and frills, they are our daily bread." And here is what Ribadeneira said of Ignatius in a classic text: "His soul overflowed in such a way with divine consolation, he found God's presence always so ready waiting for him, that he used to say that if he wanted to find God in a supernatural way ten times or more in a day, he could easily do it, but he preferred to refrain and restrain himself from such continuous consolations and drink only once a day from that inexhaustible source. In that way the body did not suffer, while the spirit gained strength, if not as much as he would have desired, at least in the proportion that was fitting for a sick and busy man as he was." These are words to set anybody thinking, words that describe and take for granted a tradition we have lost to such an extent that we take dryness as the normal state of our prayer, and some prayerful people even boast that for them it is dry prayer that counts and is considered as more meritorious and fruitful. That is an aberration on which more than a prayer life has come to grief. We have to recover the sweetness of the Spirit, the joy of his presence; we have to "taste and see how sweet the Lord is." Tony's great secret was that he knew how to make prayer enjoyable. That was the experience of a good many of us for a good many years.

Together with contemplative prayer, of which I was just speaking, Tony insisted equally on simple vocal prayer. He quoted St. Theresa, known advocate of that simplest of prayers from the heights of her own mysticism, and, more radically, the Gospel itself: When the disciples asked Jesus to teach them to pray, his answer was the Our Father. The very simplicity, humility, facility of the prayer that becomes word on man's lips is guarantee of perseverance in its use and depth in its effect. "He who cannot pray with his lips cannot pray with his heart," Tony repeated. "However much you advance in prayer," he said, "take always along with you a permanent stock of vocal prayers which you will always need in the long way." A concrete variation of vocal prayer, and a clear favorite with Tony, was the *lectio divina*, of Benedictine lineage, in its three brief stages of *lectio, meditatio, oratio*. First comes the reading of the text, preferably a suitable passage from Holy Scripture; then "meditating" on it, but meditating "with the mouth" as the Scripture says, "the mouth of the just man will meditate wisdom," that is, will pronounce slowly the sacred words, repeat them, ruminate on them, ponder them, say them aloud, taste them, feel them; and finally a brief personal consideration which is the *oratio* closes the cycle and returns to the reading. Rich and fruitful method of contact with God's word, union of mind and body in thought and phrase, humble practice and deep faith.

Then came petitionary prayer, which Tony revalued among us with unremitting emphasis. It is the prayer that calls for greater courage. Faith comes into the open, exposes itself, commits itself. It is relatively easy to recite psalms and contemplate mysteries, but when we take prayer into the street, when we make it public and concrete, when we ask aloud before others with the clarity and insistence with which Jesus told his disciples to ask for favors from the Father in his name with the certainty that they would be granted, and favors which are not only general abstract graces, but concrete help for mind and body and conflicts and problems . . . we need much more faith and serenity and Christian maturity. Petitionary prayer is not the prayer of the beginner but of the man or woman seasoned in the ways of the Spirit. It shapes us and puts us to the test. It makes us run a risk that tempers our soul and deepens our faith: If my petition is not heard, I lose face before my companions in prayer; and if it is heard, I acquire the awesome responsibility of knowing that God listens to me and takes seriously whatever I tell him. Tony used to tell the story, well known in Europe, though not so much in India, of the sick person who, after having applied for a pilgrimage to Lourdes, canceled his name, saying, "If I am not healed, well, I remain as I am; but if by any chance I get cured . . . I'll have to live like a saint for the rest of my life!" He preferred not to run supernatural risks, and remain in his comfortable sickness. It is easier to be sick than to be the beneficiary of a miracle. That is the meaning of the humorous Spanish prayer, "Our Lady dear! Please, let me stay as I am!"

After asking for favors one must give thanks, and here came the great discovery, which ruled over Tony's life for many years, that is prayer of praise. A few months after the Khandala Retreat he wrote to me a letter just for that purpose. He said in it, "Carlos, I must tell you about my latest discovery, and I cannot wait till we meet again. The prayer of praise! Try it at once, and you'll see how it changes your life as it has changed mine. Get hold of a few recent books on this matter [he mentioned some titles], and tell me soon your experiences. I would love to meet soon to talk about this. It's really good stuff." It certainly is. In *Sadhana: A Way to God,* Tony wrote, "If I had to single out the kind of prayer that has made Christ's presence more real in my life and has given me the deepest sense of being carried and surrounded by the loving providence of God, I would, without a moment's hesitation, choose this last kind of prayer which I propose in my book, the prayer of praise. I would choose it also for the intense peace and joy it has always brought me in times of trial."

Another important contribution Tony made to Indian Christian religious life was the introduction among us of the "Jesus Prayer," the rhythmical repetition in faith from lips to mind to heart of the words, "Lord Jesus Christ, have mercy on me," or an equivalent formula, together with the breath, the step, the pulse, the rhythms of our body or of the mechanical world around us. This is the meeting point of three great religious traditions: Hindu, Oriental Christian, and, through the Arabs, Ignatian spirituality. Ignatius speaks of prayer "by breathing," which is the essential trait of this kind of prayer, in the "Three Ways to Pray" to be explained for one or two days, according to Polanco, at the end of the Exercises. The Hindus have been repeating the name of Rama and the sacred syllables *"Hari Om"* from time immemorial wherever they are and whatever they do, as divine background music to their whole life, breathing the name, the faith, the love of their hearts, reciting the beloved litany on the rosary of a hundred and eight beads, writing the name in red ink thousands of times in little ruled notebooks (which I have sometimes been presented with as token of love and spiritual communion), living it out through the eternal geography of the Subcontinent from the Himalayas to the Ganges and the sacred point where three oceans meet in Cape Comorin. And, on their part, the ancient Christian monks of the Egyptian desert practiced also the repeated adoration of the name of the Redeemer, and the Greek and Russian churches have preserved the living tradition right up to our days. It was in Russia where last century appeared that anonymous classic *The Way of the Pilgrim* which a few years ago obtained great popularity in the East and the West, and led to the revival of this holy practice. This book fell into Tony's hands, eager as he always was to be abreast of anything new in the field of the spirit; there he learned himself this way of prayer, and from there he taught it to us. Today that prayer is an accepted part of the spirituality of the Indian Catholic Church, and let it be recorded here for posterity that Tony was the one who introduced it among us.

Then came what was later known as "shared prayer" or "spontaneous prayer" or simply "group prayer," that is, the silent group in a religious setting, together with the Lord in faith, with occasional readings from Scripture and singing of holy hymns, the respect to listen and the freedom to pray aloud to God as the Spirit moves each one for his own glory and the benefit of all. Tony was probably the person who introduced that kind of prayer among Catholics in India, and, in any case, he was certainly the one who made it known, and rendered it popular and universal. That practice brought a new freshness and fervor to the prayer life of groups and communities that swept through religious houses like winds of renewal. I remember wondering with friends, How is it that we didn't invent this type of prayer before? It is so simple and it works so marvelously! Now the newness has worn off, but the benefits remain. Shared prayer has become part of the religious scene in our daily life.

Tony mastered all that was best in the old and new, Eastern and Western ways of prayer, and, after practicing them himself, mastered also the art of communicating them to others. When, years later, the vicissitudes of life and the votes of the Bombay Jesuits sent him to Rome as delegate among many other delegates from the whole world, Tony

put his talents to use by offering to initiate his fellow delegates in new ways of prayer, conducting for them sessions in
English and Spanish and making spiritual contacts which
were to open to him later the doors for his worldwide apostolate. It is significant that the name he first gave his courses
was "Prayer Workshops," though their content gradually
changed into other directions. Prayer remained the starting
point of all he did.

Still, the cutting edge of Tony's spirituality was the third
point I have mentioned at the beginning of this chapter: the
practical faith that the direct experience of God is possible
in this life, and the determined effort under grace to attain it
without delay. That gave a target to the prayer of petition,
motivated the long hours of contemplation, infused the
group prayer with an intense longing, focused the rhythms
of the Jesus Prayer, and made all poverty, privations, and
hardships look easy against the perspective of that sublime
and attainable goal. Tony started his Retreats by a cold dem-
onstration carefully based on Scripture, the Fathers of the
Church, the Christian tradition, and the teaching of the
saints, that meeting God face to face in this life is not the
rare privilege of a few mystics but the birthright of every
Christian; and he followed his logical arguments by an im-
passioned plea to the effect that if this supreme grace was
open to us, how could we afford to miss the chance and be
content with the crumbs when we were invited to the ban-
quet? From then on the experience of God became the center of all our efforts and the longing of our hearts.

Tony proceeded to insult us: "What you are is 'hearsay
Christians,' aren't you? You believe because you have been
told to believe, that is all. Very nice of you. Come on, how
do you know that you are Christian? Because you can ex-
hibit your baptismal certificate? I told you: rubber-stamp
Christians. All very proper! The true Christian is a Christian
because he has seen and heard and sensed and lived Christ.

The apostle is a 'witness of the resurrection'; are you that? If you are not, you have no right to open your mouths. Are you not ashamed to speak of God in India, where only a person who has seen God is allowed to speak of him with authority? Are you children of Ignatius who expected the soul to deal 'directly' with its Creator and Lord without any kind of intermediary? Either you get in this retreat the direct experience, the personal encounter with the risen Christ, or you get nothing. Are you ready to waste one month?"

In a more sober vein I remember having thought then of the pointed definition Fritz Perls gives of the act of "teaching." According to him, "teaching is showing that something is possible." I applied that definition to my own case: Tony had shown me that the direct experience of God in this life is possible. That was the greatest favor he could ever have done me.

This unabashed approach to the supernatural did create tensions in some and even anxiety in others. Sometimes the noble endeavor took even a comic turn, and I must have laughed quietly more than once during the silences of the night group prayer when someone suddenly exploded in glorious thanksgiving to the Lord who in his bounty had heard his prayers and had manifested himself to him face to face with all his power and his love, while others who had not yet made the grade expressed their resignation and redoubled their prayers in a mixed harmony of joy and disappointment. There was here an element of friction, comparison, even competition which created anxiety and frustration and may have done harm to some. I know the theme well, and know its dangers. But the tide of fervor, enthusiasm, and genuine mystical experiences it led to was truly a new Pentecost that changed forever many fervent hearts and spread untold joy and blissful devotion through the eternal landscapes of a continent used to inner realizations and mystical upheavals. I have told the story of my own personal experience of the tide in another book of mine, and I don't repeat it here. Enough to say that I am witness, in myself and in others, to the genuineness and the depth that Tony's boldness in inviting us "to seek the face of God" carried with itself and imprinted forever in our lives.

Tony possessed an exceptional knowledge, both theoretical and practical, of the Spiritual Exercises of St. Ignatius; many had urged him to put in writing his knowledge and experience, and he himself had entertained the thought of doing so. He had only to order his files, or to tape and transcribe his talks, and edit the transcript, but he never got down to it. By the time he started publishing, his interest had shifted to other horizons.

The Writer

I have mentioned that Tony did not consider himself a writer. Yet his memory will persist and his influence will continue to spread thanks to his best-selling books in a variety of languages. Those books are essentially made up of stories, meditations, and exercises. As far as I know, Tony only once made an attempt to systematize in writing his own thought, and that was in an article he wrote in 1982 for the review *Concilium*. The title of the article is revealing: "An Eastern Christian Speaks of Prayer." Tony defines himself as "an Eastern Christian," and his topic as "prayer," and I have said just now in the last chapter that "prayer" (as in "Prayer Workshop") was the blanket term under which he developed all his thought at the given moment. He did so succinctly and beautifully in that article. As I assume it is little known, and as it is a gem on its own right, I give it here in its entirety:

1 . THE SEED

Why is God invisible? He is not. Your vision is blurred so you fail to see Him. The screen at the movie theatre becomes invisible when a film is projected on to it; so, though you ceaselessly look at the screen, you fail to see it—you are too caught up in the movie.

The Hindu meditator sits and looks at the tip of his nose, symbolising the fact that God is right there in front of us, but our gaze is fixed elsewhere in the distance. There is no question of searching and finding the tip of your nose. Wherever you go, whatever you do, awake or asleep, whichever way you turn, it is right there before your eyes. You never lose it. You only fail to recognise it.

For centuries Hindu India has seen God as "dancing" creation. The extraordinary marvel is that men see the dance and fail to recognise the Dancer.

In one's quest for God, then, one must realise that there is nothing to search for or attain. How can you search for what is right before your eyes? How can you attain what you already possess? What is called for here is not *effort*, but *recognition*.

The disciples at Emmaus had the Risen Lord right before them, but their eyes had to be opened. The scribes and Pharisees excelled in effort and failed in recognition. And mankind on the Last Day will exclaim, "You were with us and we failed to see you!" The quest for God then is the attempt to *see*.

A man sees a woman every day and she seems no different from other women until one day he falls in love with her. Then his eyes are opened and he is amazed that he could have been contemplating this adorable goddess for years and failed to see her.

Stop searching, stop travelling, and you will arrive. There

is nowhere to go! Be still and see what is before your eyes. The faster you travel and the more effort you invest in travelling, the more likely you are to go astray. People ask WHERE they will find God. The answer is HERE. WHEN they will find Him. The answer is NOW. HOW they will find Him. The answer is BE SILENT AND LOOK. (An Eastern tale tells of an ocean fish that sets out in search of the ocean; it finds no trace of the ocean wherever it turns, only water!)

2. THE ROCKY GROUND

We seek to "see" God. But do we ever see anything? We look at a new flower and ask, "What is that?" Someone says, "A lotus." All we have now is a new name, a new label, but we mistakenly think that we have a new experience and a new understanding. As soon as we can tag a name on to something we feel we have added to our store of knowledge whereas we have only added to our store of labels.

When God refused to reveal His name to Moses or to allow any image to be made of Him, He was not only proscribing the idolatry of the ancient primitive who identified Him with an image, but also the idolatry of the modern scholar who identifies Him with an idea. For our conceptual idols of Him are as pathetically inadequate to represent His Reality as are idols of stone and clay.

The word "European" tantalisingly gives you some knowledge and absolutely no understanding of this individual standing before you. You would do him an injustice if you thought that the word "European" or any other word or group of words, for that matter, gave you any comprehension of his unique individuality. For the individual, like God, is beyond all words, ineffable.

To "see" this tree, I must drop the label for it gives me the illusion that, because I have a name for it, I know the tree. More: I must drop all former experiences of other trees (as I must of all other Europeans if I am to be fair to this individual European here). Even more: I must drop all former experiences I have had even of *this* tree—we are all familiar, are we not, with the fact that we do not give this *present* individual a chance because we are constantly judging him by our *past* experience of him. Is it then surprising to learn that, if I would experience God just now, I must drop all that others have told me about Him, all my past experiences of Him and all words and labels of Him no matter how sacred? Truth is not a formula. It is an experience. And experience is untransferable. Formulas are transferable material; so they are of little worth. What has value cannot be transferred.

The word, the religious formula the dogma: they were meant to be pointers, indicators, helps to guide me in my approach to God. They frequently become the final barrier. As when I take a bus to go home and refuse to get off it when I have arrived. One thinks of so many people who go round and round in circles because they have never been taught to get off their conceptualising and theologising about the Divine; who refuse to abandon their discursive reflection in prayer and to enter the dark night, the conceptless cloud that the mystics speak of. They go through life collecting more and more labels, like the man who collects more and more material possessions that he will never use.

The river flows before your eyes and you are dying of thirst, but you insist on having a definition of water because you are convinced that you cannot quench your thirst unless you have the exact formula. The word "love" is not love and the word "God" is not God. Neither is the concept. Nobody ever got intoxicated on the word "wine." No one ever got burnt on the word "fire."

Man is more interested in the reflected than in the real. So he lives in fiction. And when he reflects on God he lives on religious fiction. He is fascinated by his concepts because he thinks they mirror the Real. His mirrors must be broken. REAL food and REAL water is needed to satisfy a real hunger and thirst. Representations of food and drink will not do. The formula H_2O will not quench his thirst no matter how scientifically accurate it is. Neither will his beliefs in God, however true. They may make him a religious fanatic, but they will not satisfy the need of his heart. (An Arab mystic tells of a man starving in a desert who sees a sack in a distance and rushes towards it in the hope that it contains something to eat, only to find it full of precious stones.) Is it any wonder that, from having failed to understand this, the Christian churches have become like exhausted mines? What is now quarried from the mines is words and formulas; and the market is glutted with these. But there is a scarcity of experience, so we Christians are becoming a "wordy" people. We live on words, like a man who feeds himself on the menu instead of the food. The word "God," the formula about God, is becoming more significant to us than the reality "God." There is a great danger that when we see the Reality in forms that do not fit our formulas we will fail to recognise It or even reject It in the name of our formulas. (A Sufi Master says, "A donkey housed in a library does not become wise. So all my religious knowledge has not improved me any more than a desert place is made fertile by the presence of a treasure in it.")

3 . THE GOOD SOIL

This attitude is best seen in the kind of divinity schools we Christians run. One would expect these schools to turn out persons who would cater to modern man's thirst for God. But they have become replicas of secular schools. They have professors instead of Masters and they offer scholarship instead of enlightenment. The professor teaches; the Master awakens. The professor offers knowledge; the

Master offers ignorance, for he destroys knowledge and creates experience; he offers you knowledge as a vehicle, only to drag you out of it when the time arrives lest knowledge impede recognition.

Secular learning is acquired through reflection, thinking, talking. Religion is learnt through silent meditation. (In the East meditation, *"dhyan,"* means, not reflection, as it does in the West, but the silencing of all reflection and thought.) The secular school turns out scholars. The religious school produces meditators. Tragically most Christian divinity schools merely change the secular scholar into the religious scholar. The secular school attempts to *explain* things and creates KNOWLEDGE. The religious school teaches one to *contemplate* things in such a way that it creates WONDER. Man has a deep-rooted Ignorance. His secular learning does not take away his Ignorance—it makes it more hidden, giving him the illusion of Knowledge. In the religious school this Ignorance is brought to the fore and exposed, for within it the Divine is to be found. But it is the rare Christian school that does this; all too frequently, the Ignorance is buried under further, religious, Knowledge.

The Christian religious school then must develop techniques to use Knowledge as a means to expose Ignorance, to use the word in such a way that it will lead to silence. Like the *"mantra"* or *"bhajan"* in India, where the word or formula is first understood with the mind, then ceaselessly repeated till a silence is created whereby the formula is transferred from the mind to the heart, and its deeper meaning is sensed quite beyond all words and formulas. Religious students must be so trained that when they read or listen to the word, their heart is ceaselessly attuned to the "wordless" which resounds in the word. They must go through a rigorous discipline till their minds are stilled and they learn, in silence, to "ponder things in their heart." (A government official asked the great Rinzai for the secret of religion in one word. "Silence," said Rinzai. "And how does one attain silence?" "Meditation." "And what is meditation?" "Silence.")

Religious students will read their Bible. But every other page of that Bible will be blank, to indicate that sacred words are meant to produce and deepen silence, a silence that is enriched by the holy words, like the rich silence that follows the striking of a temple gong. They will devote as much time to the blank pages in their Bible as they do to the text because it is only thus that they become able to understand the text. For the Bible sprang from those blank pages, from men and women who were silent enough that they could experience an ineffable Truth which they could never describe, but which they struggled to indicate and point to in words that might lead others to experience the same Truth.

4 . THE FLOWER

The Bible teaches that no man can see God and live. When the mind is silenced, God is seen and the self dies. The Masters of the East agree: When silence enters the heart, the self dies. How? Not through annihilation, but through "vision." In the stillness of silence one "sees" that the self is an illusion. The psychotic who thought he was Napoleon is healed when he "sees," realises, that his Napoleon-self is illusory. Man is healed when he "sees," experiences, that his self-as-centre, his self-as-separate is *"maya,"* illusory.

It is as if the dance were to come home to itself and "see" that it has no centre, no being apart from the Dancer; that it is not a "being" at all, but an action. Only the Dancer is Being. Only the Dancer is. The dance is not; it is-in-the-Dancer. God said to Catherine of Siena, "I am He who is— You are she who is not." When you enter into silence you experience that you are not; the centre is no longer in you; it is in God; you are the periphery. One recalls those powerful words attributed to Meister Eckhart: "Only one Being has the right to use the personal pronoun 'I,' God!"

The one who experiences this becomes Awakened. He becomes a "nobody," an emptiness, and "incarnation" through whom the Divine shines forth and acts. The poet, the painter, the musician sometimes experiences inspired moments when he seems to lose himself and feels a creative activity flow through him of which he is more the channel than the source. What he experiences in his art, the Awakened man experiences in his life. He is active, but no longer the actor. His doings become happenings. He experiences himself as doing things which are simultaneously not done by *him;* they seem to happen through him. His efforts become effortless, his work becomes play, a *"leela,"* a sport of God. Can it be otherwise when he experiences himself as a dance that the Divine is dancing, as a hollow flute through which God's music flows?

5 . THE FRUIT

When silence produces the death of the self, love is born. The Awakened man experiences himself as different, but not separate, from other men and from the rest of creation. For there is only one Dancer and all creation constitutes one dance. He experiences them all as his "body," his self. So he loves all men as he loves himself.

He does not necessarily go out in service. He knows that anyone who seeks to serve, is in danger of becoming like so many "charitable" people who are not *religious* at all; they are *guilty;* do-gooders who are always interfering with the lives of others. It is, alas, possible for you to give your goods to feed the poor and your body to be burnt and to still not have love. The best way you can be of service to the world is that YOU disappear. Then you become a vehicle of the Divine. Then service will spontaneously occur, but only if the Divine impels you to it. It might just as possibly impel you to sing songs or retire to the desert, and the whole world will be enriched by your songs or by your silence instead of being harmed by your service. ("Pardon me," said the monkey as he placed the protesting fish on the branch of a tree, "I am only saving you from drowning." Service can kill!)

In whatever you do, be it service or silence or song, you will be totally absorbed, for your "self" will no longer be in the way and you will give to each activity your whole being. This is religion at its highest. Not sitting in solitude, not chanting prayers, not going to church, but going into life. Your every action now flows from silence, from a silenced self. Your every action has now become meditation.

Christian action today is in danger of flowing from TALK and REFLECTION rather than from SILENCE. Christianity is in danger of becoming a TALKING and a THINKING religion. The Eucharist is spoken of as a CELEBRATION but has become mostly a CEREBRATION; the priest *talks* to the people, the people *talk* back to him or each other, and priest and people *talk* to God. If we would make religion a celebration again we must lessen the THINKING and the TALKING and introduce more SILENCE and DANCING. (A guru on being asked by a disciple how he had attained to God replied, "Through making the heart white with silent meditation, not through making paper black with religious composition." Nor, we might add, through making the air thick with spiritual conversation.)

The Reader

After a sample of what Tony wrote, I am going to give now a sample of what he read. I have mentioned his three favorite authors, and I am going to choose a few representative passages from all three, passages which I discussed with Tony on one occasion or another, and which had great meaning for him. If what a person reads can give some idea of what he is, this short anthology can help us to understand Tony better.

Krishnamurti's writings are backed by his life. The leaders of the Theosophical Society chose him, when still a child, to be the future messiah who was to usher in a new era of spiritual awakening on our planet, put him at the head of the "Order of the Star," and placed in his hands the leadership of the spiritual renewal at the beginning of the century. He, when the dream was about to come true, publicly renounced all honors, declared himself to be a man like anyone else, and retired to humble obscurity from which later his own gifts of intuition into the essence of being took him out and opened his privileged understanding to the world. Some paragraphs from him:

Attention is not the same thing as concentration. Concentration is exclusion; attention, which is total awareness, excludes nothing. It seems to me that most of us are not aware, not only of what we are talking about but of our environment, the colours around us, the people, the shape of the trees, the clouds, the movement of water. Perhaps it is because we are so concerned with ourselves, with our own petty little problems, our own ideas, our own pleasures, pursuits and ambitions that we are not objectively aware. And yet we talk a great deal about awareness. Once in India I was travelling in a car. There was a chauffeur driving and I was sitting beside him. There were three gentlemen behind discussing awareness very intently and asking me questions about awareness, and unfortunately at that moment the driver was looking somewhere else and he ran over a goat, and the three gentlemen were still discussing awareness—totally unaware that they had run over a goat. When this lack of attention was pointed out to those gentlemen who were trying to be aware it was a great surprise to them.

And with most of us it is the same. We are not aware of outward things or of inward things. If you want to understand the beauty of a bird, a fly, or a leaf, or a person with all his complexities, you have to give your whole attention which is awareness. And you can give your whole attention only when you care, which means that you really love to understand—then you give your whole heart and mind to find out.

Such awareness is like living with a snake in the room; you watch its every movement, you are very, very sensitive to the slightest sound it makes. Such a state of attention is total energy; in such awareness the totality of yourself is revealed in an instant.

You are never alone because you are full of all the memories, all the conditioning, all the mutterings of yesterday; your mind is never clear of all the rubbish it has accumulated. To be alone you must die to the past. When you are alone, totally alone, not belonging to any family, any nation, any culture, any particular continent, there is that sense of being an outsider. The man who is completely alone in this way is innocent and it is this innocence that frees the mind from sorrow.

We carry about with us the burden of what thousands of people have said and the memories of all our misfortunes. To abandon all that totally is to be alone, and the mind that is alone is not only innocent but young—not in time or age, but young, innocent, alive at whatever age—and only such a mind can see that which is truth and that which is not measurable by words.

In this solitude you will begin to understand the necessity of living with yourself as you are, not as you think you should be or as you have been. See if you can look at yourself without any tremor, any false modesty, and fear, and justification or condemnation— just live with yourself as you actually are.

No wonder Tony liked Alan Watts. Theologian, bohemian, Christian, Buddhist, synthesis of East and West, indefatigable talker and inexhaustible storyteller, full of wit and of life, of depth and surprise. Tony introduced me to his books, and we discussed them often. Recently I had obtained a set of cassettes with the last talks Watts gave before his death; Tony had shown interest in them, and I had promised to send them to him, but I didn't get them to him in time. Here is another quotation from an earlier book with a suggestive title: *The Wisdom of Insecurity:*

Here is a person who knows that in two weeks' time he has to undergo a surgical operation. In the meantime he is feeling no physical pain; he has plenty to eat; he is surrounded by friends and human affection; he is doing work that is normally of great interest to him. But his power to enjoy these things is taken away by constant dread. He is insensitive to the immediate realities around him. His mind is preoccupied with something that is not yet here. It is not as if he were thinking about it in a practical way, trying to decide whether he should have the operation or not, or making plans to take care of his family and his affairs if he should die. These decisions have already been made. Rather, he is thinking about the operation in an entirely futile way which both ruins his present enjoyment of life and contributes nothing to the solution of any problem. But he cannot help himself.

This is the typical human problem. The object of dread may not be an operation in the immediate future. It may be the problem of next month's rent, or a threatened war or social disaster, of being able to save enough for old age, or of death at the last. This "spoiler of the present" may not even be a future dread. It may be something out of the past, some memory of an injury, some crime of indiscretion, which haunts the present with a sense of resentment or guilt. The power of memories and expectations is such that for most human beings the past and the future are not as real, but more real than the present. The present cannot be lived happily unless the past has been "cleared up" and the future is bright with promise.

There can be no doubt that the power to remember and predict, to make an ordered sequence out of a helter-skelter chaos of disconnected moments, is a wonderful development of sensitivity. In a way it is the achievement of the human brain, giving man the most extraordinary powers of survival and adaptation to life. But the way in which we generally use this power is apt to destroy all its advantages. For it is of little use to us to be able to remember and predict if it makes us unable to live fully in the present.

What is the use of planning to be able to eat next week unless I can really enjoy the meals when they come? If I am so busy planning how to eat next week that I cannot fully enjoy what I am eating now, I will be in the same predicament when next week's meals become "now."

If my happiness at this moment consists largely in reviewing happy memories and expectations, I am but dimly aware of this present. I shall still be dimly aware of the present when the good things that I have been expecting come to pass. For I shall have formed a habit of looking behind and ahead, making it difficult for me to attend to the here and now. If, then, my awareness of the past and future makes me less aware of the present, I must begin to wonder whether I am actually living in the real world.

After all, the future is quite meaningless and unimportant unless, sooner or later, it is going to become the present. Thus to plan for a future which is not going to become present is hardly more absurd than to plan for a future which, when it comes to me, will find me "absent," looking fixedly over its shoulder instead of into its face.

This kind of living in the fantasy of expectation rather than the reality of the present is the special trouble of those business men who live entirely to make money. So many people of wealth understand much more about making and saving money than about using and enjoying it. They fail to live because they are always preparing to live. Instead of earning a living they are mostly earning an earning, and thus when the time comes to relax they are unable to do so. Many a "successful" man is bored and miserable when he retires, and returns to his work only to prevent a younger man from taking his place.

This, then, is the human problem: there is a price to be paid for every increase in consciousness. We cannot be more sensitive to pleasure without being more sensitive to pain. By remembering the past we can plan for the future. But the ability to plan for pleasure is offset by the "ability" to dread pain and to fear the unknown. Furthermore, the growth of an acute sense of the past and the future gives us a correspondingly dim sense of the present. In other words, we seem to reach a point where the advantages of being conscious are outweighed by its disadvantages, where extreme sensitivity makes us unadaptable.

Under these circumstances we feel in conflict with our own bodies and the world around them, and it is consoling to be able to think that in this contradictory world we are but "strangers and pilgrims." For if our desires are out of accord with anything that the finite world can offer, it might seem that our nature is not of this

world, that our hearts are made, not for the finite, but for infinity.
The discontent of our souls would appear to be the sign and seal of
their divinity.

I came to Bertrand Russell through mathematics. I stud-
ied the three thick volumes of *Principia Mathematica,* in
which, through a language of symbols, he strives to prove
that mathematics is formally nothing else than logic; I enjoyed his famous definition that "mathematics is the science
where we do not know what we are talking about, and we
do not care whether what we say about it is true"; and I told
many people, including Tony, Russell's paradox on "the set
of all sets" which caused an upheaval in mathematical circles, and which Russell himself explained in this way in popular form. In a small village with only one barber, the barber shaves all those men who do not shave themselves.
Nobody has a beard. Who shaves the barber? If he shaves
himself, he cannot shave himself, because he is the barber,
and the barber does not shave those who shave themselves;
and if he does not shave himself, he has to shave himself,
because the barber shaves those who don't shave themselves. If that is not a tongue twister, it is a brain twister,
with serious consequences for the theory of the philosophical foundations of mathematics.

Tony liked to quote to us, already in Sadhana I, the "lib-
eral decalogue" of Bertrand Russell, with its ten principles
of intellectual honesty and mental health which fitted exactly into Tony's own thought. Here I prefer to quote another page, which is one of the writings that has touched me
most in my life. It is the prologue to Russell's *Autobiography,*
and is as follows:

Three passions, simple but overwhelmingly strong, have governed
my life: the longing for love, the search for knowledge, and unbear-
able pity for the suffering of mankind. These passions, like great

winds, have blown me hither and thither, in a wayward course, over a deep ocean of anguish, reaching to the very verge of despair.

I have sought love, first, because it brings ecstasy—ecstasy so great that I would often have sacrificed all the rest of my life for a few hours of this joy. I have sought it, next, because it relieves loneliness —that terrible loneliness in which one shivering consciousness looks over the rim of the world into the cold unfathomable lifeless abyss. I have sought it, finally, because in the union of love I have seen, in a mystic miniature, the prefiguring vision of the heaven that saints and poets have imagined. This is what I sought, and though it might seem too good for human life, this is what—at last—I have found.

With equal passion I have sought knowledge. I have wished to understand the hearts of men. I have wished to know why the stars shine. And I have tried to apprehend the Pythagorean power by which number holds sway above the flux. A little of this, but not much, I have achieved.

Love and knowledge, so far as they were possible, led upward toward the heavens. But always pity brought me back to earth. Echoes of cries of pain reverberate in my heart. Children in famine, victims tortured by oppressors, helpless old people a hated burden to their sons, and the whole world of loneliness, poverty, and pain make a mockery of what human life should be. I long to alleviate the evil, but I cannot, and I too suffer.

This has been my life. I have found it worth living, and would gladly live it again if the chance were offered me.

Role-Playing

Back to Lonavla. After seeing Tony at work in the different roles he played during his life, I want to focus attention again on his definitive role at his last Renewal in Lonavla, and on a particular activity of his during those days. Tony was never dull, but fifteen days of exclusive show could tax anybody's powers of concentration, and Tony thought up means of lightening the show without remitting from its intensity. His main resource for that was "role-playing."

He was a master at it. He could spend from one to two hours role-playing without a letdown of attention for a moment. The procedure was simple, and always the same. He would assume a particular role, usually of a priest or Sister with a concrete problem, give himself a fictitious name and address himself to any man or woman in the group asking for advice in his situation. He always began his role-playing by addressing himself to a Sister in the group called Tina, so that when he started, "Tina, I'm an old priest; my name is

Frank, I . . . ," we knew that role-playing had begun. Then the whole group took notice and sat up. There was going to be no passive listening, but anyone could become an active player at any moment. The rules were simple. Tina could counsel Tony (or Frank) for as long as she wanted, and could pass him on to anyone else in the group if she so desired at any time. If she was reluctant to do this (which she usually was, and Tony teased her for that on the last day), anybody else could jump in and take the job from her hands at any moment, and so on from hand to hand. Then suddenly came the turning point. Tony without previous notice would switch roles and say, "Tina now you are Frank, and I am Tina; you urge on Frank's problem, and I'll counsel you"; and so again around the group. We sat in a circle, so that everybody could see everybody's face, watch reactions, and be ready for intervention. There were surprises, insights, laughter, pathos, silences, and even tears, but never a dull moment. Tony's role-playing was an outstanding learning situation.

Tony's powers of spontaneous reaction were so great that he countered every answer to his problem with a further aggravation of it, so that after a few rounds of counseling his situation looked much worse than at the beginning till it became truly hopeless. It was then that he switched roles, and, applying again his talent and his wit he turned the tables and made the solution appear natural and obvious. It was quite a performance, and I never got tired of watching it and taking part in it. What I cannot do is to reproduce on paper what I lived in person; but I can list the roles he played and the problems he chose, together with the lines along which the discussion proceeded. His selection of topics and characters is already significant, and the few hints gathered from those long sessions can be helpful.

One important warning. The very fact that Tony chose role-playing to deal with these questions shows that they are not streamlined problems with a ready-made, clear-cut solution, but rather situations to be described, states of mind to be understood, ways of approach to be suggested, knowing only too well that the person will have to carry his burden, and hoping only to lighten it with genuine understanding and personal warmth, learning all the while ourselves how to cope with those situations in our own life as they crop up sooner or later in one way or another. Role-playing is not a logic class but a school for life.

Another warning. Tony's choice of topics may appear limited and one-sided. This has an explanation. All of us in the group were old Sadhana students, which meant that most of our obvious, universal, personal problems had been dealt with at length in our respective courses, and so they will not appear in the present list. On the other hand, the topics here are all the more interesting because they are more general, actual, and chosen carefully by Tony after much reflection, as he himself said. They also show his courage and sincerity in bringing into the open some conflict situations which are usually hushed up and glossed over in official circles. This is to me one of the great services Tony rendered the establishment during his life: respectful awareness from the inside of the problems of our institutionalized way of life, and sensitive readiness to talk about them with people equally concerned about them. Having said this, I now proceed to describe most of the actual role-playing that took place in our Lonavla meeting.

"Tina, I'm an old priest, past seventy already, my name is Frank, and, well, there is nothing seriously wrong with me. I've had a long life as a priest and I hope that is in God's books already, but, you see, I honestly find myself totally useless now. I can do nothing of what I used to do, in fact I am a burden to myself and to others; yes, people are kind and put up with me and even greet me with respect when they pass by my side, but for the rest they ignore me and leave me alone; and, you see, I find myself not only useless but unattractive, I mean even physically unattractive. My face is all crumpled up with wrinkles, I cough often, and, well, I realize it is not pleasant for people to be near me. This has made me lose my self-respect. I feel humiliated while saying it, but, yes, I hate myself, at least I despise myself, and so I am now in a constant depression which, I guess, will end only in my tomb. Still, I've heard that you are a good hand at helping people who feel low, and so, not without a good deal of hesitation, I've come to you as a last resort. Can you do something for me?"

Tina tried her best. So did all of us. And at every attempt old Frank was sinking deeper and deeper into his own misery. When someone told him, "Remember the good you did to others in past years," he countered, "That makes it even more painful for me to see that I cannot do it now." When someone else exhorted him to think of heaven, he smiled sadly: "By then I won't need your counseling anymore." The case was hopeless. When Tony took it up he agreed that it was too late to do anything substantial for the man, but he took the opportunity to point out that what had ruined him was the "O.K. approach" to life. He had felt fine so long as he could do something and be somebody, so long as he was O.K. in the eyes of the people and therefore in his own eyes. He had identified himself with his work, and now that his work was gone, so was he. The lesson was to get out of the O.K. trap at the earliest, and to realize that my worth does not lie in my work but in my person.

"Tina, I'm a Jesuit Provincial. I'm doing a good job, and I'm appreciated both in my Province and in Rome. I can go on cheerfully till the end of my term, but there is one point that troubles me. You see, Tina, I don't mind telling you because you are discreet and I know you won't tell anybody, and then there is the professional secret of the counselor and all that, so I feel safe with you and I don't mind telling you, and on the other hand I have to tell somebody because I need help in this, and I think you are the best person to help me in this situation. Well, the point, Tina, is that I am an agnostic. I feel relieved to see that you are not shocked to hear that. Yes, of course, you have met other religious who have serious difficulties with their faith in one degree or another, and I too have quite a few of them in my flock. There is nothing new or strange with that. In fact I, personally, feel quite comfortable with my situation and it does not cause me problems in my own life. It is not, of course, that I deny the existence of God or the divinity of Christ, simply that I don't know, and so I think I owe it to myself to be honest and not to force myself into believing what I in fact do not believe. It is a kind of respectful doubt and a consequent inhibition of judgment, and I feel quite peaceful in that situation. My problem comes from my job. I am the Provincial, and I feel uneasy at being an agnostic superior in a religious order. See, one of my priests was not saying Mass, since, as I told you and you know by yourself, some of our men have their own doubts in the matter of religious faith and practice; but now the authorities in Rome have been informed about it, and they have asked me as Provincial to persuade that priest to say Mass again to prevent a scandal among the faithful. Now, how am I going to persuade him to say Mass when I don't believe in the Eucharist myself? But that is not exactly my problem. What I want to consult you about, and the point on which I want your concrete guidance is, should I resign as Provincial or not? You see, I could go back easily to my previous job. I was teaching chemistry in a school and I can continue to do that happily without much of a religious problem, and, again, if I apply to Rome to be relieved from my job, I need not tell them the real reason. I know how to put things in such a way that they will grant me what I want without really knowing why, so I could easily get out of public office and back to my standing as an ordinary priest. The question is, should I?"

The all-around counseling brought out a number of points. The question was not academic. Faith has come to be an issue with us, and only harm can be done by ignoring it. Radical solutions are no solutions. We read now books by serious Catholic theologians with ecclesiastical approval, which say things that we in our student days were taught to be heretical. There are limits, of course, which cannot be tolerated, but there is a large area where honest doubt can coexist with genuine commitment. We can help the doubter more by understanding than by pressure. Great prudence is necessary in dealing with others, and nobody should impose his doubts on people who don't have them. Though, again, nobody should impose his rigid views on people whose views are not so rigid. Some people advised the agnostic Provincial to relinquish not only his job but also the exercise of his priesthood, if he wanted to be honest with himself; while others, on the contrary, were of the opinion that he could be of greater help to people in similar crises by remaining in his post. Tony intervened: The Provincial can be helped by understanding that the Bible, the Eucharist, the Magisterium, even if they are not objects of faith for him now, are in any case pointers to something, and he'll be wise to heed gently the message of tradition even if he does not bind himself to it with the bonds of obedience. Skepticism is as bad as dogmatism. The wisdom of the ages can be ignored only at our own cost. On the other hand an honest doubt can be more pleasing to God than a forced belief. Let him keep himself open and advance step by step in his own way with humility and gentleness. And, Oh yes, one warning: If anyone comes to you with "proselytizing experience," that is, quoting his own religious experience to impose his views on you, simply switch off; his experience was his, not yours; he may be mistaken, for all you know, and there is no way of finding out. Treasure your own views, but never impose them on others. And don't consider yourselves better than anyone simply because your credo is longer than his.

"Tina, I'm a religious engaged in social work for many years. I wasn't doing that before, you know, but then all this wave of the 'option for the poor' came along and I felt sort of conscientized, and discovered, what I already knew, that there was a slum of poor people next to our religious house, and I began going there, getting interested in them, doing things for them. They didn't have running water, you know, and they had to walk half a mile to the nearest tap, so I organized them and we fought it out all the way to the municipality, and I got them a water connection, which was a great relief, though I never thought they thanked me enough for it, but never mind that, we are supposed to work for God alone. And then, yes, I got a medical van with a doctor and a nurse to come for them twice a week, and, well, things of that type. But now to come to the point. I've gone of late through a kind of spiritual experience, well, I don't know how to call it, there's a crazy guy, Tony de Mello, maybe you know him, and I went through one of whatever he calls those things he does, and, well, yes, I've realized that after all everything is transient, yes, transient, and so now back in my place I think, if the problems of these people are after all transient, why to get involved in them? I still go there, but not with the interest I had before; they've lost their water connection and are back to the old tap, and, well, I'm not going to go through that whole thing again; in a word, I've obtained peace of soul but they've lost their running water. And then this idea that the only way for me to help others is to grow myself, the only way to liberate others is to liberate myself first, and I'm working at it, and that is fine, isn't it? And also, some of these social workers do more harm than good and even seek their own interests and use the poor for their own advancement, which I am sure must be true in some cases, though of course not in mine. But all in all I've lost interest, and I'm thinking of dropping the whole thing, for which, to be honest, I never quite felt real interest and I see this now. Though on the other hand I feel a kind of remorse to leave those people to themselves, I am afraid of what my companions will say about me, and I don't know where I stand and what I have to do. Can you help me?"

I give directly Tony's reaction. If anybody ever thinks that by coming to Sadhana he is going to lose his interest in working for the poor, let him come and see! The reluctance some social workers have felt to come to Sadhana, and the definite slander Sadhana has had to suffer at the hands of a few such people who have never come to it, may precisely show that they are in special need of it. We all, in whatever kind of work we may be, need to examine our intentions and purify our motives, but perhaps social workers are the ones who need it most because of the power they wield and of the masses they control. Work for the poor is sometimes undertaken out of a sense of guilt, thirst for power, peer pressure, need to conform to prevailing ideals, compensation for inferiority complex, escape from a long intellectual formation. All that, where it exists, has to be purified before going to the poor, or else social workers will do more harm than good as they hiddenly and subconsciously pursue their own interests, using for them the very people they propose to serve. I don't hesitate to say that Sadhana is the best preparation for work with the poor: It purifies workers from their own mixed motives, and it makes them freer, which is the only way to communicate freedom. And now for the matter of all suffering being "transient" and therefore not worthy of our attention. That is pure theory, and here we are learning to react to facts, not to theories. If you see a child suffering and you know that you can stop his suffering by giving him an injection, will you not give it on the plea that his suffering is transient? If you see an old lady stumble down the stairs, do you not instinctively grab her and prevent her from falling, rather than philosophizing that after all the fall is transient and this too will pass? Follow your instincts, not your brains. The trouble with people is that they interpose their Christian vision or Buddhist dream or Marxist plan, they don't see the poor anymore but their own plans and start "activities" to bring about their "conceptions." Let us work for the poor by all means, and let us work out of our own free selves, not out of hidden needs or secret compulsion.

"Tina, I'm an Indian Sister of a rather conservative congregation, and that, of course, brings in some problems now, you understand, chiefly for some of us who want to follow the modern trends and be closer to the people, and so we had been discussing it very long, and some were in favor and some against, and other congregations had changed already and we were not allowed and I felt ashamed when Sisters of several congregations met in Retreats or seminars, and some of them were wearing sari, and mind you, not uniform sari, but just any sari some of them, not white or blue or brown for all, but any color they wanted, and some in very good taste, and I felt jealous and angry against our own superiors who did not allow us to wear sari, and finally all the Indian superiors of our congregation got together and after much discussion they agreed to ask our Mother General in Rome to allow the sari for us in India, and, imagine, she has refused, and we have to wear our habits, and you see what old piece of clothing they are, do you see it? Don't laugh, please; it's not funny. And, well, I'm very angry with Rome for this and for everything. Are we not an Indian Church? Is there not such a thing as inculturation? What do they know there of our needs here? And what gets me down is that the men can do whatever they want. Look at those Jesuits, they dress in any way they choose, while we poor women are subject to the whim of people we don't even know. And to make it worse, they have now forbidden us to speak about it among ourselves. I feel ashamed to have to speak so before you who are wearing such a beautiful blue sari with crosses on the border, but I hope you'll at least understand me and sympathize with me, won't you?'' (Tony had been imitating throughout the voice and gestures and mannerisms of a woman while speaking, and it was difficult to keep a straight face listening to him and watching him. His acting was always part of the show.)

The matter of the sari was easily disposed of. Sister was told, You have a choice; either to conform to directives and shelve your protest, or to put on a sari and bear with the consequences. Make your decision and stop fretting. The matter of inculturation was tackled by Tony. He had a great love for India, and he had shown it in a practical way, among many others, by his decision to accept only priests and Sisters working in India (with very few exceptions) for the ''maxi-Sadhana'' for the last few years in spite of the many applications that came from abroad; but he rejected the narrow aspect of patriotism, and said so bluntly in this case. ''If you think as an Indian, or as a European or an American, you have stopped thinking; because then you think only from your conditioning, which is not you.'' He had no use for accidentals. Culture, not as art and knowledge but as imposed heritage, was also a conditioning, and therefore to be transcended.

"Tina, I'm a Jesuit priest, and I have a delicate problem which I hope you, as a woman, and a very intelligent and sensitive woman at that, will be able to understand, and so to give me some guidance in it. I am really perplexed and I am suffering a lot. By the way, my name is John, and I want you to call me just by my name. The fact is, Tina, that for many years I had a deep friendship with a Sister, Jane, and I truly loved her and she loved me, in a very pure way, of course, everything absolutely aboveboard, without chemistry if you know what I mean, which you surely do, and that went on for quite a long time, and she was by far my best friend, different from all the other women I knew, and she was fully aware of it and corresponded with her best love to me; I was her man and she knew it and loved no one else the way she loved me. But then, Tina, a few years ago Jane was transferred to another town—you know how it is with you Sisters, all of you have convents all over India and are transferred for no reason and without notice—and there she landed in the other corner of the country, and I, of course, remained where I was. We wrote to each other, and her letters showed and continue to show that her affection for me remains intact, that she is as faithful and devoted to me as she was when she lived here, and that, of course, she takes for granted that such is the case with me too. But there comes the trouble, Tina, and I hope you will understand. Not that I don't love her, I certainly do and try to reassure her in my letters, but, well, yes, I see you have guessed it already, it's true, another woman has come into the picture, and things have changed for me. She is a Sister from another congregation, and her name is Mary. We became friends, and I saw nothing wrong because I still loved Jane more and thought it would always remain that way. But it hasn't. I didn't want to admit it to myself, but it was evident, and now it is a fact I cannot deny. I love Mary now much more than Jane. Now see whether you can follow the tangle of my feelings. I feel guilty to love Jane less, and I wish it were not so, but I can't help it. I have always prized very highly the virtues of loyalty, fidelity, chivalry . . . and there you have me now letting down the first woman I've loved in my life while she continues to worship me. You can imagine how I feel about myself. My self-respect is in rags at the moment. Of course, I haven't told Jane about Mary, and, well, no, I haven't told Mary about Jane either. Do you see the tangle? I keep writing to Jane, and every letter is a torture to fake feelings and hide facts. How long can I go on? Should I give up Mary? Should I give up Jane? And if I choose Mary, what guarantee do I have now after this experience that later will not happen with Mary what has happened with Jane? Then should I give up both of them? But that is hurting both, whereas in the other way I hurt only one. And the fact is I am unable to hurt any of the two. And I am afraid the more time passes, the more I'll have to hurt them. Now, you are a woman; can you give me some light in the midst of this confusion?"

That was by far the longest and most beautiful role-playing we had in all those days. The whole group participated in it for the best part of two hours, and since there were men and women among us, roughly half and half, the tact, delicacy, thoughtfulness, and sensitivity of all the proceedings were moving and exquisite. Tony, after taking John's part, took also by turns Jane's part and Mary's part, each time bringing out new angles of the intimate webs of feelings, love, and friendship. Without solving any problem, much light was shed on the affective life of religious people with its gains and its dangers, its fulfillment and its loneliness. We all had much to learn that day.

"Tina, I'm a parish priest in a rather conservative parish, and yes, by age and by tradition, quite on the conservative side myself. I came to India as a missionary, you know, many years ago; I am a foreigner, though I love India as my country, and I've worked hard for many years to do the best I know and could, which was to make people Christian and baptize them. Yes, you know the story, they were mostly poor people of low caste, and I helped them with gifts and money I got from good Catholics in Europe and America, and so they were grateful to me, and to please me and get more help they became Christians, and I know people call them 'rice Christians' or 'bread-and-butter Christians,' which is very bad; but after all they are Christians, which is the main thing, isn't it? And the Lord has his ways to call people, and even if one generation becomes Christian for selfish motives, the next will become a genuine Christian generation, and who, after all, ever acts out of only pure motives, tell me? And so I was happy in my missionary work, and counted the increasing number of my converts with pride, and happily sent my statistics to Rome, and was congratulated every year for my zeal and my apostolic work. But then came all this new theology of the Vatican Council, which upset me very much. You see, I had based all my efforts and justified my ways on the dogma that 'outside the Church there is no salvation,' and, of course, God has his ways of mercy, but by and large Christian baptism is the best way to heaven. And now the Council says in so many words that even an atheist can go to heaven! So where do I stand? What is the value of my lifework? Have I made a fool of myself all my life? To make it worse, all these young priests, natives of the country, denounce our work as spiritual colonialism, and want us foreign missionaries to quit and go back to our countries of origin. I feel quite confused and even resentful. To my great pain and frustration, groups of old Catholics in my parish also reject the new low-caste converts, and deplore the lowering of the standards of the faith. I personally feel angry when I hear all this talk about ecumenism, and Hindus who can be saved in Hinduism and Muslims in Islam. I feel it is my duty in conscience to resist all that and come back to the purity of the faith, and I never go to prayer meetings with Hindus and Muslims and don't let my parishioners go. We have to preach a holy crusade against the enemies of the gospel, haven't we?"

I vividly remember this role-playing because I took a specially active part in it. I was no match for Tony's wits, but this time I was inspired and in a good mood, and got even with him. When after much fencing he said, "I do this in duty bound as a good Catholic," I retorted, "In that you are not a good Catholic, not even a good Christian; what you are is a good Muslim preaching a holy war on all the infidels!" Tony parried the attack by looking mildly offended and then posing the practical question, "Call me what you want, but what am I to do?" To which my answer came fast: "If you are honest . . . go and get yourself circumcised at your earliest convenience!" The group burst into laughter, and that was the end of the role-playing.

"Tina, I'm a Sister in charge of the promotion of vocations for our congregation. We are a team and we work much from school to school and almost from village to village trying to attract girls who may come to know our life and eventually join the novitiate. It is getting harder and harder to obtain vocations. But what is harder for me is to define now where I stand. You see, I have come to question the propriety of my job. Not that I question my own vocation—I'm fine where I am, and in any case it's rather late now for me to change direction in life. But I ask myself, Am I really happy? Are the Sisters I know truly happy in the religious life? Officially we all are, and we all smile when they take photos of us for the propaganda magazines. Also, if you ask me, as a matter of faith we are in the best possible position in this world with a view to the next. All that is fine. But, well, you are also a Sister and you'll understand me. When I know the misunderstandings and jealousies and pettinesses and infidelities to our vows and frustrations inside our own religious houses, what right do I have to go and persuade those young girls to come and join us for life? I know a Sister who in her own family has dissuaded her younger sister from joining. And knowing what she has gone through, I cannot blame her. True, married life is not a paradise either, but then nobody makes propaganda for people to marry, while we do it for them to become religious. I feel quite uneasy about it. Shouldn't we rather leave people to their own desires, and, if nobody joins us, take that as a sign that we have to change the type of religious life we live and try new ways of living our vows and our consecration in consonance with the needs of the new world? Formerly we had vocations in plenty without pushing anybody, because our life responded to a need in the youth of that society. Should we not now find the needs of society today and then build up a religious life that appeals to the new People of God?"

The question was serious, and, undoubtedly, it would have given rise to a fruitful discussion; but unfortunately it came at the end of a session, and there was no counseling nor feedback. I shall not invent it here either.

"Tina, I am Judas and you are God the Father. I have come to you for my reward. Yes, don't look at me with that expression of surprise. My reward. After all, I did your job for you pretty well, didn't I? Of course, anybody else could have done it, I agree, but you chose me for it, and I did it with all care. Yes, your job. Without it your whole plan would have gone flat. No redemption for mankind, and no glory for you. It was an unpleasant job, I agree, but precisely for that I deserve greater credit. Anybody is ready to play king on the stage, and nobody to play villain. But without the villain there is no play. Without me there was no Passion, and without Passion there was no happy end for your Salvation History, which is what they now call your play down there. Yes, yes, I know that I got paid already, everybody knows about the thirty pieces of silver and they have rubbed it in enough for you to repeat it again. What I want now is my rightful place over here to enjoy my retirement together with all the other actors of the play. We all did our part, and in the end it came out well, didn't it? You needed me then, and I did my bit to oblige. Now, please, get Peter to open that gate and let me in. I know that man Peter, nice fellow, and he too did a couple of darkish scenes in the play, and there you have him now in charge of the show. Just a word, and we'll get all the old pals together. I knew you couldn't say no, but thanks anyhow. And if you ever need me again for whatever part, you know I'm always ready. Any accountant needed up here in heaven?''

That was Tony's favorite role-playing. I saw him go through it on more than one occasion. His point was to underline the role that circumstances and conditioning play in our lives, so that what we do is to a large extent the result of the framework in which we live. He always liked to tell in this connection a story he had heard in Spain. Holy Week is tourism time in Andalusia, with its processions, sculptures, singing, and exhibitions. Part of the yearly celebrations in a certain Andalusian village is a public act of thanksgiving to Pontius Pilate. The reasoning is faultless. Without Pontius Pilate there was no Passion. Without Passion there was no Holy Week. Without Holy Week there was no tourism. And without tourism there was no income for the village. That made Pontius Pilate a benefactor of the village, entitled every year to the solemn vote of thanks by the mayor in the central square. And entitled too, by Judas' own account, to a place with him in glory in the company of all the actors of the divine play.

All of Tony's readers know that his favorite quotation was the one he put at the end of his first book, *Sadhana: A Way to God,* from the mystical vision of Juliana of Norwich: Christ on the cross laughed "right merrily" and told her, "And all thing shall be well; and all thing shall be well; and all manner of thing shall be well."

Unencumbered by Baggage

When Tony questioned me about my interviews with Krishnamurti, and we talked about them, one point came up with particular sharpness, as it appealed strongly to both of us and we enjoyed talking about it. The idea was not new, and we both had come across it in his writings, but it acquired a new freshness as a word-of-mouth experience, and we lingered with mutual pleasure over it.

Krishnamurti had told me, "When I go for those long daily walks of mine, alone through the woods for one or two hours, it happens to me that not a single thought crosses my mind during all that time. Yes, I know, psychologists say it is not possible, but there you are, it happens to me. I must be a freak!" He smiled winningly as he said the word "freak," he asked me whether I knew what it meant (I was reminded of his insistence never to go on talking unless he made sure that what he had said had been understood), and then went on. "I have also a similar experience at night. I sleep well, and I never dream. Again psychologists say such a thing is not possible, but it is in my case." Then he came to the vital point: "I think this happens to me because I enter fully into each experience, and I come out clean from each of them too. I put the whole of me into all I do, and . . . out of all I do. Nothing sticks to the mind, and maybe that is why it remains clean." He said no more on that point, but I sensed at the moment that he had said something of the utmost importance.

Tony, who lived this idea on his own, insisted on it repeatedly and beautifully in Lonavla. Live every experience to the full, so that it leaves no residue in the mind. No leftover, no remainder, no scraps. Account without carryover. Journey without luggage. No living on credit, but cash down each time. In and out; fully in and fully out. Again the lotus and the water, the symphony that flows, the river that runs its course.

What prevents us from living this way (which is the only true way to live) is attachment on one side and fear on the other. We are attached to an experience and we don't let go of it in our minds even when the experience has already passed; or we are afraid of a coming event, and its fear fills the mind before it has arrived. A free mind carries no encumbrance. A free mind lives life moment to moment, and this is the secret to enjoying it to the full.

Tony not only spoke like that, he also lived like that. One little insight he gave in passing in one of those days. The Lonavla grounds were large and were divided into two parts: the old grounds, where the St. Stanislaus Villa stood, and where the Sadhana Institute had been housed for several years, and the new grounds, a portion cut out from the old, separated now by a wall, and where the new quarters for the Institute were being built. The two grounds being contiguous, we often passed from one to the other, and it was in this connection that Tony said one day in the group,

"It's curious what happens to me, but I've observed it again and again. I often pass through the old Sadhana grounds where I lived and worked so many years with the intensity you all know, so that those grounds and every corner in them are full of memories of all kinds for me. I know all this, and I remember all this, and yet the fact is that whenever I pass through those grounds, in company or alone, I feel absolutely nothing by way of emotion, attachment, romance, or nostalgic feeling. Nothing. And I am not a stone, as you know. I feel deeply. But nothing stirs in me when I go through those grounds. The reason must be that I lived that experience to the full, and it has left no residue within me. That is the way I want to live."

That was the way he lived. And he left a signal testimony of it in the last words he said to us in Lonavla, which will also be the last words of this book. Inspired farewell, pathetic parting, prophetic benediction at the end of the final Eucharist we offered all of us together in thanksgiving to one another, to Tony and to God.

It was the last evening of the last day, thirteenth of April 1987, Monday in Holy Week. The Eucharist was almost over in the same hall and with the same chairs that had witnessed so many intense and beautiful moments in those truly blessed fifteen days. We were lingering lovingly and unhurriedly over the deep silence that followed the passing around of the paten and the cup with the Body and Blood of Christ who held us now all together in the embrace of his presence and his love. In that sacred silence Tony spoke, and these were his words:

"Don't change. Desire to change is the enemy of love.

"Don't change yourselves: Love yourselves as you are.

"Don't change others: Love all others as they are.

"Don't change the world: It is in God's hands, and he knows.

"And if you do that . . . change will occur marvelously in its own way and in its own time."

He paused for a while and he added his final words:

"Yield to the current of life . . . unencumbered by baggage."

He did.

ABOUT THE AUTHOR

Carlos G. Valles, S.J., is a Spanish Jesuit priest who has
worked in India for the last thirty-eight years, and became a
close friend and associate of the late Father Anthony de
Mello, S.J. He has written dozens of books, for which he has
received India's highest literary award as best prose writer.
His book *Living Together* is distributed in America by the
Institute of Jesuit Sources and *Sketches of God* by Loyola University Press. In addition, his work has been translated.